"Catching Tongues is a brilliant and important book, on three levels. It is a fascinating personal story, an invaluable guide to parents who want their children to have fun whilst acquiring essential bilingual skills and a marker for Government and LEA's as to how to avoid the disastrous slump in the numbers studying modern languages."

- Dr Martin Stephen, High Master, St Paul's School

CATCHING TONGUES

How to Teach Your Child a Foreign Language
- Even If You Don't Speak One Yourself

By Carolyn Gibson

ISBN: 978-1463600617
ISBN 13: 1463600615

Cover art & interior illustrations by Paul Wilcox
Cover by Joleene Naylor

Manufactured/Produced in the United States

Table of Contents

Foreword

My inspiration for starting to teach my children a foreign language was my parents: my father, who speaks two languages fluently and can get by in at least six more; and my mother, who is Dutch and thus, almost by definition, speaks four languages fluently.

My mother never spoke to us in Dutch at home but language was all around us: in visits from my *oma*, in dictionaries lying around the house, in travels abroad, in the friends my parents brought home. It was not atypical to find a Greek alphabet book lying around the house, or a German phrasebook, or Russian poetry. My mother always had an English dictionary at hand to look up words she didn't recognise. Although it was not until I was twelve that my parents embarked on a grand scheme to immerse their children in French for a year, I grew up nursed by the love of languages, and to this day credit that alone with my ability to write, read and comprehend English in a much more rounded way than many people with an equivalent education. And, incidentally, the enthusiasm for languages pushed me to travel and to study French, Dutch, German, Russian, Serbo-Croat and Mandarin.

It is by no coincidence then that I sincerely believe in nurturing a love of language in my children from the very earliest age. Language learning does not just open up new horizons with people and cultures abroad; it does not just create a wider world vision; it does not just help counter narrow nationalistic viewpoints. Language learning improves the connections in the brain itself, making learning English easier; improving the ability to grasp concepts and ultimately giving your child a claim to confidence and uniqueness that he or she will carry through adulthood.

Nevertheless, I have to say that I didn't start it with my first child until he was over two years old. Even with all the linguistic advantages in my upbringing, I still didn't know how. I did not grow up bilingual; my husband is not fluent in another language. Where do you start if the words for baby bottle, pacifier and nursery rhyme don't naturally trip off the tongue? My tourism-centred French vocabulary was not at all helpful!

Eventually, I bought my first French nursery rhyme CD, book and DVD. Through a bit of research and a lot of trial and error, I am now firmly on the road to helping my children learn French, in the most fun, most exciting and yet most unobtrusive way possible. I want my children not just to gain a language, but indeed to grasp the enthusiasm and excitement that I feel for language learning. It is this enthusiasm that will carry them farther than I could ever carry them myself.

Now I would like to help other people who may be interested but, like me when I was starting out, lack the information and the tools, to have the confidence to make a start. It is a long journey, but all the little, surprising, delightful language steps your children take will make the effort worthwhile.

If you find this guide useful, you may wish to check out www.languages4yourkids.com to gain insights from other parents who are trying to help their children, and to access some of the materials referenced here.

Good luck, and have fun!

Advance apologies

In this book, I have consistently used "he" to refer to an individual child. This is partly because I found it onerous to switch from "he" to "she" in politically correct regularity, and partly because I have two young boys and am unconsciously referring to them much of the time.

I also switch, inconsistently, between child and children, for the same reason. No one ever said authors had to be completely logical.

Although I try my best to be even-handed when it comes to languages, I generally refer to examples in French, as that is the language I am using with my boys.

Finally, as I live in England I have used UK English spelling and terminology.

If you have a single girl child, and would like to teach her a language other than French, and live in North America, I apologise in advance. I sincerely believe however that you will still enjoy and learn from this book, so please read on!

1. An introduction to this guide

The problem

From a young age I planned to meet the man of my dreams - a tall dark European of an unspecified country - at age 28, marry him at age 30, have children starting at 32, and raise my children to be bilingual. As it turned out, I was unbelievably accurate in my predictions. I proposed to my European boyfriend at 28, married him at 30 and had my first boy, James, at 32[1]. The only problem was, my boyfriend, now husband, is British.

And while my boys, James and Scott, enjoy making fun of my American pronunciation, and say "fart" with relish in the US, and "trump" with enthusiasm in the UK, that is probably as far as their "bilingualism" in those areas will ever go (thank goodness!).

I do have a working knowledge of French, and a smattering of other languages under my belt. Nevertheless, when James was born I realised that while I could try to speak only in French with him, it would put an enormous strain on the already exhausting experience of having a newborn baby.

What finally occurred to me, when Scotty was born, was that just because I didn't speak a foreign language to them all day every day didn't mean I couldn't help them learn a foreign language. It was simply a matter of choosing one, sticking with it, and building up slowly, together, a fun and yet consistent way of exposing them to a new language.

Curiously enough, no one requires you to have a degree in mathematics to teach your children about numbers, or a PhD in English to teach them about letters. A foreign language is no different, and yet the expectation is still that somehow, in this field, we have to be experts. This guide sets out to dispel that myth.

Bilinguals[2] - people who speak two languages fluently - have the opportunity to provide a 'home immersion programme' for their children in which day-to-day conversation plays a pivotal role in the learning process. People who are native speakers of one language, living in a different language community, for instance English speakers living in Germany, have a similar opportunity.

As an English-speaker married to another English-speaker living in England, my husband and I do not have the luxury of having more than one language on tap for our children. And, to add insult to injury, the majority of books I've read on the subject of teaching languages to young children are written for bilinguals!

This guide is meant to bridge that gap. It is a distillation of everything I've researched and tried out on my own children, and it effectively proves that children can easily learn a language without having a bilingual parent to guide them.

Shall I say it again? You don't have to be bilingual to teach your children another language. You can do it - no matter how much or little you know. And if you are bilingual, but find the "all or nothing" approach suggested by most other authors difficult, better to try "little by little" than none at all. This guide will help you to do it - and to have great fun along the way.

It's catching

Young children are hard-wired to learn language. As infants, they listen carefully to the sounds you make. Within a few months, they already try to copy those sounds (that lovely stream of ta-ta-ta's and ba-ba-ba's). Eventually, sometimes as young as two, they are making short sentences, and working out grammar along the way. As Colin Baker, an eminent advocate of bilingualism, wrote, "Language among young children is caught rather than taught." [3]

How true!!! Trying to stop your child from catching the latest lingo is like trying to stop them from catching the cold that is going around the nursery. Your mission - if you should choose to take it on - would be to allow some of that lingo to be a second language.

This guide focusses predominantly on the experience of helping younger children (ages 0-8) "catch" a second language - a second tongue. Ideally, children should be exposed to a second language from birth. This is because from six months onwards, children slowly lose the ability to distinguish sounds other than their native tongue, so the wider the range of sounds they hear, the more likely they are to be able to mimic those sounds when they begin to speak. This is one of the reasons why those who learned a language after adolescence have more difficulty in picking up the correct accent - they can't hear it properly in the first place. Another reason to start very early is that making sounds with our vocal chords, throat, tongue and lips is a complicated business which requires a phenomenal amount of training: training that our children unconsciously undertake when they are babies and toddlers.

The age ranges up to 8 years old because it is around this age when children naturally become more independent and more self-conscious. A child pre-8 years old is more likely to take your word for it. A child pre-8 years old is more likely to have fun learning pronunciation and new words, without any concern for how it sounds to their own ears, let alone friends and family. A child pre-8 years old has not yet learned that learning isn't supposed to be fun. This book suggests strongly that if you can get your child over the language learning hurdles before age 8, you will substantially reduce painful negotiations and resistance later on.

So it is natural for this guide to focus in on language learning from an early age. However, as anyone knows who has tried to teach pre-school children and those in early primary years, a young child's learning style is very different from older children and adolescents. This book focusses to a certain extent on a way of - rather surreptitiously - inserting language learning experiences into a young child's everyday activities. It is not a manual for formal learning - it doesn't give exercises or lesson plans - it is rather a guide to having fun with your children, with a second language as the backdrop.

Certainly, the philosophy of this guide is that language learning should be about having fun and building confidence. Baker talks about building your child's "language ego." It is about communication, not correctness; about the journey, not the destination. If anything, helping my boys learn French helped me let go of my own need to have everything come out just right, in favour of just delighting in every little exchange I have with them.

The language advantage

One of the reasons why I think I am successful at teaching my boys languages is my unwavering enthusiasm. However I admit that I am the type of person who is enthusiastic about all learning. I make table mats of the solar system so that James can name the planets over breakfast, help Scott zoom into Google Earth and explore the continents, count the steps two-by-two on the way up to bed, and change the music in the CD player in a way coldly calculated to expose them to classical, jazz and West End tunes. The poor fellows know nothing but information overload!

If enthusiasm is the key to helping your children learn, then theoretically an enthusiastic oboe player should teach their children about music; an enthusiastic nurse might teach their children about biology and the human body; an enthusiastic mechanic might teach their children about planes, trains and automobiles. Unfortunately, there are only so many hours in the day, so for a football-mad family, football practice will often take precedence over piano lessons, and a family outing to the Saturday game will take precedence over a trip to the planetarium. We just can't do it all.

The advantage of language teaching is that it is something that can easily be done *alongside* any other pursuit, without detracting from it, or straining the already jam-packed family schedule. For language is the medium for learning, as well as the end. The vocabulary is different - you say "*un*" rather than "one", and "*gardien*" rather than "goalie", but the concepts are the same[4]. As an example, my son had some homework set in which he had to figure out what the heaviest thing in the house was. It is fairly easy to do this in a second language - you introduce the word "*lourd*" (heavy) and go off on a hunt for things that are *lourd* - "*le lit*" (the bed), "*la table*", etc. James learned the concept of heavy and (incidentally) some French too!

So there is no need to balance language learning against any other pursuit - just add it in, like a new spice to your favourite stew, and see what happens.

2. Why teach your child a foreign language?

When your first child is born, you are bombarded with advertisements and shop shelves full of toys, games, books and CDs to help them learn. You feel forced to buy special pictures to help your infant learn to focus their eyes; DVDs that introduce counting, and cuddly bears that spew out colours and numbers in symphonic tones. You begin to get the idea that you are not only responsible for feeding, clothing and cuddling this child: you also are responsible for making sure that their minds grow along with their cute little toes.

Now as a responsible parent you have to make choices, and often we focus on the obvious: helping our children learn pre-maths and pre-reading basics. The problem is, children's minds develop at different rates. Their readiness to learn numbers and letters will vary from child to child, with some NOT being ready for either numbers or letters until way past their third birthday.

Learning the language basics - to listen, understand and speak - is something that ALL children are hard-wired to learn from the earliest age - earlier than maths, earlier than reading. Children begin to understand what we say at a minimum by the time they turn one, and start trying to speak shortly afterwards. As world-renowned linguistic scholar Steven Pinker points out, it is no accident that children begin to understand and speak at the same time they start to be able to walk. Language is a matter of life and death.

So if you have the desire to teach your child something - anything - at an early age, then a second language is actually the easiest choice. If that is not enough for you, here follows some of the academic, social and political reasons why I think all children should learn a foreign language from an early age.

Academic advantages

Improved sound perception. Studies show that when babies are born they can perceive all the sounds around them; however in order to communicate, they have to learn to screen out the sounds that are not relevant and focus in on the sounds they need to decipher and use. Babies exposed to English sounds such as "r" will learn to hear and repeat those sounds; Babies exposed to Spanish sounds will learn to hear and repeat the rolling "r". From six months old therefore their sound perception begins to slowly decrease, to the point that from adolescence it becomes very difficult just to hear a new foreign language properly, let alone pronounce it well. And without hearing it properly, it is nigh on impossible to speak it properly.

So if all I did with my children was expose them to French sounds from an early age (in addition to English), then I would have already done a tremendous amount to improve their ability to pick up French at a later stage in development. (Incidentally, this is why I categorically deny those reports that say that watching television in another language is useless; yes, children do not learn how to speak, but nevertheless they learn how to hear!) Improved speech pattern and intonation perception is also part of this osmosis period in childhood. The first thing a French person says when they hear my boys speak French is that they have a perfect accent - and that is no accident. Having the right accent is important - it helps you fit in immediately, even with a limited vocabulary. Isn't that yet another thing we want for our children - to fit in, wherever they go?

General language development - grammar and vocabulary. Children exposed to other languages early on learn very quickly that there are different ways of communicating, and that these are governed by different grammatical rules. Grammar therefore becomes a much more concrete concept which thereby allows improved manipulation of sentences, even in English. Similarly, any Roman or Germanic language learned will have vocabulary that is similar or related to English vocabulary. Just learning one of these languages automatically increases your English vocabulary. I remember being quite upset when some visiting French friends managed to correctly state the meaning of more English words in a major English exam paper - serious words like capricious and indigenous - than I could! They easily understood the meaning of English words from their French derivation.

Improved school enjoyment and exam results. In the United Kingdom, a statutory entitlement to learn a foreign language in class time is being introduced for 7-11 year olds in 2011. This means that if your child is in the UK he or she will be learning a second language in school. Now, as involved parents we strive to make sure that our children do not fall behind in numeracy and literacy, and yet many of us hardly take an interest in their language learning. Yet this is a significant part of their day that they will have to get through. Why not make it easier for them by providing them with the basics earlier?

In secondary school, the stress faced by children taking exams is horrendous. One way to make it easier is to guarantee them an excellent mark in at least one exam - a foreign language. They can learn the language, play with it, enjoy it - all from an early age before they are even aware they are learning - and then use it to improve their exam results later on.

Improved mental agility. When my Scottish husband and I first moved to Birmingham, England, it was I who had to translate for him from the Brummie-ese spoken by the locals. This was simply because my language training had made it easier for me to pick up on one or two words and use them to make sense of whole sentences. The inevitable code-breaking that people naturally use to learn languages can translate into improved mental acrobatics in a variety of fields. In a similar way, language learning is excellent training for long and short term memory retention, which can be used in all sorts of fields, including history, law and science.

Development of an interest in and enthusiasm for words. Learning a new language allows you to explore different ways to express the same thing, or alternatively, different ways to express subtle nuances. Even simple things, such as colours, mean very different things in different languages. My children take great delight in being able simply to name an item in a different language, and will shout out *"camion"* when a lorry goes by, or wonder what "slide" is in French, and ask me to look it up in the dictionary. This interest and feeling for words can naturally translate into a more creative approach to writing later on.

Understanding the distinction between concepts and labels. Some studies of bilingual children have shown that these children have improved understanding of concepts as distinct from labels - for instance that the word cow is an arbitrary label distinct from the concept of a cow. If we all agree to call a cow "dog", then the cow concept is intact: only the label has changed. This mental distinction allows greater freedom of thought, and increased creativity, when problem-solving. I was always one to try to change the rules of any game and my early exposure to the "arbitrariness of labels" might be the culprit! [5] Scotty is in the middle of developing his own language "Stonish" and enjoys giving me a new word for a randomly chosen household item at least once a day.

Development of motivation to learn foreign languages. We all know that motivation is what makes the difference between success and failure in any endeavour. You can be gifted in maths or talented in music, but if you don't have any real motivation to learn, then these gifts and talents are simply wasted. For this reason, I don't hold much stock in "talent". Motivation is what counts - a deep desire to learn. Motivation is what happens when practice - gentle, fun practice - leads to success. You can wait until your children reach the age when they will take French lessons in school, and see if their motivation for learning takes off then. Or you can build success through practice into their daily

lives now, and then when they start languages in school, they will hit the ground running.

Development of motivation to learn foreign languages. We all know that motivation is what makes the difference between success and failure in any endeavour. You can be gifted in maths or talented in music, but if you don't have any real motivation to learn, then these gifts and talents are simply wasted. For this reason, I don't hold much stock in "talent". Motivation is what counts - a deep desire to learn. Motivation is what happens when practice - gentle, fun practice - leads to success. You can wait until your children reach the age when they will take French lessons in school, and see if their motivation for learning takes off then. Or you can build success through practice into their daily lives now, and then when they start languages in school, they will hit the ground running.

And motivation in language learning leads down a very interesting path. Once a child has even partially acquired their first foreign language, it becomes much easier for them to acquire further languages. As they understand how it feels to switch from one language to another, this huge barrier vanishes. For this reason alone it is (almost) inconsequential which foreign language is chosen for the first one, as children will, as interest or necessity leads, learn others, especially those in the same language group as the first. As an example, once my five-year old son learned that our DVDs did not only play in French, but other languages, he often requested another language - *Polski* this time, *Italiano* another. He seemed to enjoy trying to pick out words he understood. Magical.

The 10,000 hour rule. The 10,000 hour rule is the current accepted wisdom that people who are experts at something simply have put in more hours working at it. If all it takes is for your child to put in the hours to learn a language, then why not start clocking up the hours earlier rather than later? Why not start before they reach an age where learning becomes a chore? Just one hour per week from birth means that by the time your child reaches the age of seven, the age they are

required to start languages at school, he or she would have put in more than 350 hours of learning time: more language training than they will receive in the whole of their school years.

Incidentally, it is perhaps no coincidence that children are deemed experts in their native language at the 3-4 year point: 12 hours times 365 days times 3 years equals just over 10,000 hours.

Social and personal advantages

Development of confidence. If there is one thing all parents would like to instill in their children, it is confidence. From confidence flows improved work and social opportunities, and for most people increased happiness. One almost fool-proof method of instilling confidence in children is to help them to become very good at something. Many people choose sport, which has the benefit of being good for the mind and body both. Nevertheless, because of the number of people involved in sport, it is difficult to find one in which children can excel to the point of being able to be better than most of the people around them (without the effort detracting from their overall childhood experience, anyhow).

Learning a language however can make us stand out from the average person quite quickly. For instance, James's teacher noticed his French ability already at age 5 and developed a part in the annual nativity play to allow him to sing a short solo in French (what a great teacher, eh?). I have no doubt that otherwise he would have not had a speaking part - only because of his French, he had a starring role. He reveled in it (and so did I!). In a class of bright pupils, he can still stand out, be recognised and be rewarded.

Don't just take it from me however. Extensive research has shown that people who have pleasant language learning experiences from the outset develop greater self-confidence in speaking in a wide variety of contexts, partly as a result of lack of anxiety about speaking a foreign language and partly as a result of their developing competence. [6]

Insight into culture. Learning languages inevitably brings some basic knowledge of native customs. Different customs can be truly eye opening, especially for young children. Did you know that there is no tooth fairy in France? Instead, little mice take away your tooth in the night. That in Holland, St Nicholas comes on 5th December and fills up your wooden shoes, not your stockings? With these little lessons comes the knowledge, sometimes very difficult to shift in older people, that indeed there are many ways of doing the same thing, and that they are not necessarily worse than our own - only different. Vive la difference!

(There are of course some risks in giving children too much knowledge. After one December afternoon we spent together going through a little poster with all the world's different Christmas rituals, James looked up at me suddenly and said "mum, they're all wrong aren't they, because it is always Santa who delivers gifts on Christmas Eve, isn't it?" I had a bit of trouble trying to explain my way out of that one!)

Combating societal xenophobia. Sadly, even in this day and age of global integration, I am almost daily hit with evidence of xenophobic views of society, all held as a result of ignorance. It is clear that somehow normal, otherwise quite nice people are afraid of people who seem foreign: the South Asian consultant who tends their wounds; the Polish immigrant who just might steal their job; the American company who takes over "a good British firm." No one seems to be able to explain to me what makes a British stranger somehow more trustworthy than a foreign stranger. We are all human beings in the end.

People who learn another language and have a chance to converse with people of other nationalities as equals tend to treat them as equal, rather than as "the other". As parents, I believe we have a duty to raise our children to be citizens who will ensure that racist, xenophobic ideas are not tolerated in our society, and learning a second language is one way to help our children down this path.

Travel, study, social and work opportunities. Many people are afraid to travel to a country where they do not speak the language. Removing the linguistic barrier for even one country seems to encourage travel almost anywhere. Regarding study, apart from having improved results to be able to gain entrance to better universities, it is also possible to consider studying abroad - and ultimately working abroad. With just one extra language even only partly learned, the world suddenly becomes easily accessible: truly your child's playground.

Fun. One of the best games to be enjoyed when traveling is to go along with the assumption natives make that you do not speak the language - which allows you to innocently eavesdrop in to the conversations that go on around you. I was treated to an excellent story in French about a woman's experience of dating an English bloke, all while standing at a car rental desk in the Geneva airport. Then there are the endless complaints about tourists.

On a chair lift with my husband on the last ski holiday, the French teenagers next to us proceeded to berate the greedy Brits amongst themselves, and then began a tirade against the fat Americans ("land of hope and calories" was the comic phrase of the day). At the end of their litany of complaints one of them said "I hope they're not American" and my husband promptly replied, with a big smile, "She is, and she's not that fat!"

Removing personal and social barriers to language acquisition. For us English speakers, it is accepted "wisdom" that Chinese is a difficult language to learn. Chris Lonsdale, author of the book *The Third Ear,* remarks however that this is a myth: "If a billion or more Chinese people can speak Chinese, it can't be that hard...."[7] He passionately believes that people develop early in their lives barriers to learning languages that persist into old age. These barriers include the myth that learning a language is hard, or that it is a talent rather than a learned skill.[8] Such psychological barriers can seriously undermine older children's (and adults') efforts to learn a language. Starting a child on the path to learning a second language earlier in their lives easily avoids this potential psychological issue. As Lonsdale notes, "The people who have mastered more than one language simply believe they can, and refuse to accept any excuse. Because they know that the myths about 'difficulty' or 'impossibility' are just that. And these myths can make it seem harder to learn than is really the case."[9]

Another psychological obstacle many people have acquired from their school days is that a second language is a "taught subject", e.g. that it is best learned in school. Nothing in fact could be further from the truth. Indeed, most children in England will have learned to speak near grammatically perfect English by the age of four - before they go to school. And those in China will have learned Chinese to a similar standard - before starting school. In fact, the ones that learn language at school stumble more frequently - trying to remember taught rules of grammar, or translate in our heads - instead of simply using language the way it was intended - to communicate our needs, and get other people to react in a way that meets them.

This is another reason to try to learn a second language at an early age: the language used with children is simpler and more directly tied to their immediate needs and surroundings. Language courses for adolescents and adults regularly feature such difficult subjects as global warming, politics and social ills - subjects that in effect must be learned from textbooks because they are as distant from the immediate needs as can be.

Indeed, some research suggests that where we are in the best frame of mind to use any new knowledge is in the place where we learned it. So if we want to be able to speak Chinese in the classroom, learning it there is very appropriate. If we want to use it for our everyday lives, learning in a classroom is actually somewhat counterproductive.[10] Living the language - at home, with our loved ones - avoids this stumbling block.

The fact is, we can achieve all these academic, social and personal goals by helping our children *outside of school*. But first, we need to address those who do not understand language learning - we need to silence the sceptics.

Enter the sceptics

There will be some people who argue that learning a second language is not good for children. They argue that the children suffer confusion and a lack of vocabulary in their main language. Intuitively, I find this hard to understand.

In terms of vocabulary, children will learn what they are exposed to. A word-rich environment is more likely to create a word-rich child. A natural interest in words is the first indicator in the long-term development of vocabulary. If a child is expected to learn that both settee and sofa are slight variations on the same object, then why not add "*le divan*" to his or her vocabulary? All of a sudden, the word divan in English is then accessible to the child. Learning a language is ultimately vocabulary-enriching rather than impoverishing.

Some will argue that children will mix up their vocabularies, speaking both languages in one sentence. My own children both did this, but no one seemed to mind, and by age four they had mostly grown into the understanding of when and where to speak which language. What is the harm if they do mix a little, for a while? In many languages the vocabulary and grammar varies depending on whom one is speaking with - use of the formal and informal in French (*"vous"* and *"tu"*) and German (*"Sie"* and *"du"*) is a case in point. Eventually children learn when to use *"vous"* and when to use *"tu"* - without thinking about it. Similarly, children learn instinctively which language is to be used when.

Bilingual parents sometimes find that their child might encounter problems with their internal rules on when to speak a language - for instance, if they have deduced that "all mothers speak French and all fathers speak English". Initial confusion is created when they realise that this is not the case, but it is quickly replaced by the internal rule, "my mother speaks French and most others speak English". As adults we have to adjust our internal rules from time to time as well. For instance, having grown up in Vermont, my internal rule was that all mountains are covered in trees. When I drove through the Pennines in northern England for the first time, I realised my internal rule had to change to include "except those sheep-strewn bald mountains up in Cumbria." It must be noted that no one was harmed in any way in the remaking of that rule.

Some otherwise enthusiastic parents have shied away from teaching their child a language if the child is already struggling to keep up with their normal schoolwork. Certainly there is no evidence to show that learning a second language detracts from learning a native tongue, and as I mentioned before ultimately it is an overall advantage. I can only think that perhaps parents might find the stress of helping their child with their schoolwork causes them to cut down on extracurricular activities. Integrating language learning into daily routine - for instance to bathtimes or mealtimes - should help ensure that it doesn't detract attention from schoolwork.

The most difficult criticism I deal with is the "hothouse" parent issue: people who feel I am force-feeding my children language and that they suffer as a result. The positive side of this criticism is that it makes me ensure that learning for the children is always fun, engaging and exciting. When asked about his language "homework" the other day, James forcefully corrected the inquisitor: "It's not *homework*, it's a *game!*"

As in any aspect of child-rearing, it is important not to let others' issues and doubts get in the way of how you want to raise your children. A little conviction can go a long way.

This is not to say that some parents encounter problems in teaching their child a second language. Indeed, we all encounter problems when trying new things - that does not mean they are not worth trying! Chapter 7 of this guide deals with some of these problems.

To understand better why language learning is so important at a young age, the next step is to look at how children learn their first language. It is only from there that we can best understand how to teach our children the next.

Chapter 2: Summary

Why teach your child a second language?

Academic reasons include:

- Improved sound perception
- General language development
- Improved exam results
- Improved mental agility
- Development of an interest and enthusiasm for words
- Understanding the distinction between concepts and labels
- Development of an interest in foreign languages
- The 10,000 hour rule

Social reasons include:

- Development of confidence
- Travel, study and work opportunities
- Insight into culture
- Fun
- Removal of barriers to learning

Less informed people might try to tell you that learning a second language:

- retards primary language development
- leads to language mixing
- takes up time that should be devoted to other areas
- is something only "hothouse" parents do

Ignore them! They haven't read this book.

3. How children learn languages

Before you get started in teaching your child a second language, it helps to understand how your child learns languages. I have put a whole chapter in here because learning a language is not like learning numbers, or letters, or anything else for that matter.

As an example, both James and Scott went through a stage at about 3 years of age where they would confidently state that "Dad be's upstairs" and "he is the good-est football player". They were grammatically correct actually - except that the "to be" verb is irregular, as is the development of "good", and they hadn't learned it yet. No matter how gently and no matter how many different ways I might rephrase it -"Oh, Dad *is* upstairs" or "who is the *best* football player"- this language "mistake" happened for months. Then, one day, without me realising it, they figured out that "is" and "best" are used instead. On the way to learning languages, everyone has to make mistakes. It is a natural and necessary part of the learning process.

The tendency that we, as adults, have learned ourselves is to teach (meaning for the most part 'correct') in a formal way. Ironically, this tendency is even more pronounced for things we know less about, e.g. a second language, *for that is the way we learned it* (which explains why we are so hopeless at it sometimes). Language however is not learned. It is absorbed. It is caught.

To be excellent language teachers, we need instead to provide a rich language environment, and let the children pick out the lessons for themselves. My boys had learned an excellent lesson - that the 3rd person singular verb normally has an "s" added to it. Unfortunately, they had to unlearn it for the verb "to be", and it wasn't for me to unlearn it for them. I could only provide lots of opportunities for them to hear the word "is", in lots of different contexts. We control the environment, the child controls the learning.

In *The Language Instinct*, Steven Pinker has written an in-depth analysis of how children learn language. Reading his book, I have found it fascinating to understand what my children are going through when they are learning. It also helps me figure out what in the environment I might need to tweak to help them learn. If you are in a bit of a rush, or less interested in the mechanics, then by all means feel free to skip most of this chapter and move right along to the summary at the end. If you have time, it is worth reviewing the information below because it will help you understand your child better - and make you more patient.

Pinker's main contribution to the debate[11] about language learning is his assertion that babies are born with brains that are already set up to learn languages quickly. This effectively means that all children have a language framework hardwired into their brains that allows them to hear, decode, store and retrieve words (vocabulary), as well as to structure sentences in a way which creates meaning (grammar).

If we look at it in chronological order, there are three main stages of learning a first language:

- Learning to understand, at 0-12 months, when a child is absorbing the language around him;

- Learning to speak, at 12-36 months, when a child begins to speak and pick up grammar; and

- Practice, practice, practice, from 36 months onwards, when a child builds vocabulary and refines his use of grammar.

For learning a second language, the steps are very similar even if the timing is different. Indeed, in depth studies show that each language is learned in a series of steps peculiar to that language, no matter whether it is your first language or your fifth. [12]

Understanding that there is a sequence - a learning path - that your child will automatically follow, if there is enough language stimulation, is the first step. It should give parents the ability to relax and enjoy the process, rather than experiencing a driver's anxiety about controlling the outcomes.

Stage 1: Learning to understand

When a child is born, he already has a language that he uses: the language of thought. This language of thought is related in a direct way with what is happening out in the world, and consists of concepts (vocabulary) and relations between concepts (grammar).

Babies for instance already have a concept for food. They taste a banana, and associate that with a kind of nourishment (the brain has an inbuilt categorisation function). They then hear the sound ba-na-na, which eventually they can distinguish from other sounds, and then eventually associate that word with the concept they have of banana. Bit by bit, in this way, they build up a vocabulary related to their inner concepts.

To do this effectively, babies need to be able to decode what they hear, and link it to an internal concept. Surrounded by sounds, from 6 months onwards they start to hone in on the sounds of speech. If they are surrounded by English, they learn to hone in on English sounds. Eventually, the nerve connections in the brain that allowed them to hear and hone in on other sounds, such as the Spanish "r", wither away from disuse. They simply don't need those connections, and instead are building ones that help them with English.

Then they have to link the sound to the internal concept. It is no good just saying the sound "banana" over and over again: the baby only learns what "banana" means when you give it a banana, or take away the banana, or point to the banana. The child needs to interact with the word directly. Research suggests that it can take up to 16 "encounters" with a word to finally remember it to a level of being able to recognise it in a new context, and even more for being able to retrieve it and use it in speech. [13]

What does this mean for the child learning a second language? Firstly, it means that the child needs to be exposed early to the language sounds - oodles of them. Secondly, it means that it helps enormously if listening to the sounds is accompanied by something with which the child interacts. Television and songs are great for exposing a child to early sounds, but your choices must be ones that are clearly spoken and easily understood through non-verbal clues, or ones where you are there with the child to provide the clues yourself.

It reminds me of the situation that I've found myself in periodically, where I think I am making great strides in learning a language and then become gravely disappointed when I cannot understand the nightly news broadcast in that language. With quick speaking and little visual clues, the content and meaning is lost. If you expose your child to a second language, think about how clearly the words are spoken and how easy it is to figure out what each individual word means.

Babies - indeed, all of us - need to hear a great deal of sounds before they can make out recognisable language patterns.[14] The more we expose our children to relevant, child-friendly language, the more able they will be to decode the babble into words and sentences.

Stage 2: Learning to speak

Children start to babble before they turn one year old, but at first they are not copying words; they are training their sound-producing organs which include the vocal chords, throat, tongue and lips. Pinker identifies six different parts of this sound production factory which can all interact to create thousands of different sounds. English uses about 40 of these sounds - apparently slightly above average. In short, babies have to work hard to train their bodies to create these very specific sounds.

Unsurprisingly, they don't spend much time learning how to create sounds in other languages. As a child ages, it becomes more and more difficult to create these different sounds as by a certain age most children (or adults for that matter) do not want to spend 4 to 5 hours a day babbling away just to try to mimic a particular sound. Much better to get that vocal training in well before self-consciousness kicks in.

Have you ever listened to a child babble on and on with nonsense words, and remarked on how much it sounds like real speech? That is because a small child is learning to reproduce not just individual sounds but the full intonation and rhythm of the language. And every language's rhythm and emphasis is so different. Emphasis in words is crucial to understanding. For instance, say the sentence "He is important" aloud. Now say the same sentence, putting the emphasis on the syllable "im" of important, instead of the usual "por" emphasis. Even if you pronounce the word "important" correctly, the emphasis creates the sound of the word "impotent". Through no fault of his own, the man in question has gone from a position of strength to, well, a medical issue. Again, intonation and rhythm is much easier to pick up as a child than as an adult.[15]

Now that the toddler is on his way to reproduce sounds, he moves very quickly to trying to produce meaning. Producing meaning first requires being able to produce words - and out come their first words. A 15-month old might have six words in her vocabulary, with approximate pronunciation that probably only mum and dad understand: mum (person), ball (object) up, hot (descriptions) and bye and no (social interactions). As toddlers grow, they pick up more words in each of these categories.[16] I will come back to this list later in this book, as it is relevant to what you might consider introducing to your children in the second language.

There is a bit of a debate on how children best learn these words. Some of it is imitation, but often of the baby sort: playing with the word on the tongue, making sure it sounds right. As an example, Scott loves to play a vehicles card game on the computer in French. Every time he picks up a card during this particular game, a voice says *"un camion"* or *"un bateau"*. And he repeats it, loudly, clearly and completely unconsciously. Again, it just feels as though children are hard-wired to do the right things - e.g. practicing how to say words out loud - that will make them language experts.

Another aspect of learning a word - as opposed to just playing with the sound - is identifying it in a sentence. Many people suggest that pointing and saying isolated words like "banana", "up", "yes" helps the child isolate the meaning and then use it. Also emphasis helps the child learn the word "do you want to go DOWN?" or "NO, you can't have that cookie."

A final aspect of using words to produce meaning involves learning grammar, because it is grammar that allows us to relate concepts. "Want milk" is a huge step from just saying milk, because all of a sudden the child can not just identify something, but ask for it specifically.

For me, this is where language learning gets interesting because children have an innate sense of grammar. What they do is they hear a sentence "I want milk" and use their inbuilt grammar framework to deposit "I" into the subject category, "want" into the verb category and "milk" into the object category. Their brains expect these categories: most languages categorise things in the same way. But what their brains don't know yet is the order: Subject-Verb-Object, or Subject-Object-Verb, or Verb-Subject-Object, to name a few. Once the child hears enough examples, his brain will automatically jump to the conclusion that the language he is learning is Subject Verb Object, and the child will start to arrange his own speech that way - even if he hears examples from time to time which contradict that. [17]

As a baby, all word orders are acceptable. One is then picked up, and this is enough then for this word order to be strengthened, at the expense of any other.

For the purposes of second language learning, this gives us a fantastic insight into how our children learn best. First, we need to give them a minimum set of vocabulary. Then we need to give them the opportunity to hear both individual words and full grammatical sentences (ideally shorter ones first) as much as possible, to slowly build the nerve connections between subjects and objects and verbs in a way that allows them to embed the second language's grammatical structure.

And we need to do it early on, for two reasons: firstly, because if we can build up our child's second language vocabulary at the same time as the first, or nearly at the same time, then the child avoids the unnecessary extra step of translating from the language of thought into English and then to the second language - especially when differing word orders make such translation challenging.

Secondly, it allows children to fully embed a second grammatical structure in their minds, before it can conflict with the structure of their mother tongue. How many of us, learning a second language like French or German, struggle with the word order? This is because we have learned to expect the adjective to come before the noun ("blue dog" as opposed to *le chien bleu*) or the verb to come before the noun ("I can see that" as opposed to *ich kan das sehen*). Let the children learn the alternative structure before their expectations become obstacles.

Pinker notes that "as far as grammar learning goes, the child must be a naturalist, passively observing the speech of others." A child does not try something out, wait for a reaction from others, and then figure out whether it was right or not. It is his own brain which just seems to "know", from listening to hundreds of hours of speech, what is right. The more they hear, the better they get. [18]

It is personally a relief to me to learn that children don't learn grammar simply by completely mimicking me and only me, or by waiting for me to approve or disapprove. They learn by listening to a wide variety of language, applying their internal grammatical rules and coming up with something *that just sounds right.*

It is not that children don't imitate - as I mentioned before, imitation is helpful for honing sound production - pronunciation and intonation. It is true that initially many children do use imitation for this. But imitation is not a core part of their learning process, and indeed many children learn without much if any imitation. Children are far more creative than that. They are amazingly adept at identifying patterns of speech and then adapting them to whatever situation they need. So it is patterns that they pick up on and patterns they copy - not individual words and phrases.[19]

Children are forever comparing what they have just said with what they think it should sound like - both the accent and the grammar. They use their own internally built rules to compare - they don't only use you. Chris Lonsdale compares this type of learning to a tuning fork [20] - the child can hear the perfect language in his head - a perfect language gleaned from patterns identified in hundreds of thousands of different examples - and just has to practise saying it.

In effect, it is not necessary to correct your child. It may even be counterproductive. Rephrasing isn't even necessary. The most important thing for your child is to gain confidence in speaking: with practice comes success. With enough input, they will learn on their own. You just need to be patient.

Stage 3: Becoming a language genius

Once the basic vocabulary has been built up, and a basic understanding of the grammar rules of that particular language, children's language development begins to take off. This is because with an understanding of just a few words, and an understanding of the relations between the words, decoding the meaning of sentences

becomes easy. If I picked up a book and held it out to you and said "xx you xxxx xxxx book?", you could already figure out that I probably am asking you if you want it or have read it. This is at once amazing and entirely normal.

From the point of view of helping your child with a second language, this move from memorising words to learning how to decode is the goal. Because decoding is a skill that a child can practice on their own within a rich language environment. And it is not a hard target to aim for. With a starting line up of 100 or so words, a child can quickly start to build up their comprehension - filling in their language gaps themselves.

How quickly, you might be asking. Well, studies suggest that by the end of secondary school most people know a minimum of 20,000 words. This means children and young adults learn as much as 10 new words per day[21]. To understand how astonishing our brains are to be able to do this, Pinker compares it to memorising 10 new phone numbers every day. Ten phone numbers! I can't even remember my own number half the time. Something about our brain makes it unbelievably easy to learn *words in particular*. This capacity has developed because words are important for our survival: if you say to your child, don't touch it, it's "hot", then you quickly learn one way or another not to touch something that is "hot".

Core words such as "hot" - basic, necessary vocabulary for everyday life - only number a few thousand in most languages. So this means that for basic, everyday conversation, we actually only need to aim for our children to learn maybe 2000 words.[22] But let's face it: we are not going to sit down and make them memorise 2000 words. Instead, they "catch" the vocabulary through decoding sentences they hear day in, day out.

To allow them to achieve this level of decoding, it is important that what we offer our children is relevant to their lives. Most language manuals are geared to what is relevant to adults, and school textbooks really only start targeting older children from the age of 9 or 10.

Younger children have different needs and the language they learn will reflect their needs. Pinker quotes Lily Tomlin: "man invented language to satisfy his deep need to complain." [23] Listen to what your child says in English. What does he complain about? ("My tired!" says my nephew Teague). What is his passion? My older son picked up sports words first - *la balle* (the ball), *le foot* (football), *le but* (goal). My younger one loves food - and picked up *le chocolat chaud* as his first French words. What does he say in the morning when first getting out of bed? What does he notice when driving in the car? What does he say over tea at night?

Of course, we have come across some funny situations when for instance a French word is used in English as an English word, and my sons have learned it in French first. James recently went over to a friend's house, and had the household in stitches. Apparently every time the mother offered him a croissant, he corrected her pronunciation! No, it is *croissant* (emphasis on the second syllable, no "t" sound) not croissant (emphasis on first syllable and "t" sound at the end). Of course she said it over and over, and I of course was mortified that he was so adamant in his corrections. My friend thought it was hilarious.

It is important to be aware that, in developing their language genius, different children will focus on different parts of the language. When my brother and I went to school in France, we used to hang around together whenever possible in the beginning to support each other. If a child spoke to us, I would translate it into English for my brother, and he would reply in French. He enjoyed the communication - I enjoyed the translation. Similarly, James does not like to say anything unless it is absolutely correct, but as a result will pay closer attention to what he learns; Scott is happy to come out with anything as long as people respond. Neither focus is better, and in the end both my brother and I achieved a reasonable standard in French in the end, and so will my boys. We all have different ways of getting there, that's all.

Lonsdale, a vocal advocate of language learning at all ages, points out that all great language learners focus on language as a tool for communication. "Great language learners do not set out to learn a language. They set out to communicate with people...."[24] You need to think not about what words your child needs to learn, but what words your child needs to communicate: to get results. One of my big breakthroughs with my children was to make sure that they had the words to ask for something they wanted - and then expect them to use those words when they wanted it. It was not enough to ask for me to put the music on in the car: they had to ask me politely, in French, exactly what CD and what song they wanted. It was amazing how quickly they did it when they knew it would get them their song.

A new, more natural approach

I think that all the research to date points to a more natural approach to learning a second language. I suggest that such an approach has the following steps:

1. Build up a rich language environment. Your child will learn English by listening to it for months and months before trying to speak. Yet normal language teaching methodologies do not build in much if any listening time at all. Providing your child with early exposure to lots of sounds in the second language will be invaluable to understanding and speaking later on. This first step could be the only one you ever take, but it is one that surely puts them on a firm foundation for learning the language in the future.

In writing this book I came across some amazing research in second language learning. One study found that children learning a second language who were simply exposed to books and audiotapes suited to their level - with no conversation practice whatsoever - made *better* progress than children over the same period in a traditional school setting - *even in the area of speaking.* In other words, just listening and reading the language gave them a basic ability to converse. It suggests very strongly that comprehension is the bedrock of language, and building that bedrock should be at the core of our efforts to help our children.[25]

2. Let them take the language lead. Take the time to figure out what your children want to say; give them the words to say it; and then expect them to use those words to get the results they want. Your children use words in English to get the things they want; allow them the same opportunity in the second language. Communication needs to be the goal, rather than correct use of language. Indeed, corrections are only necessary as a means of clarifying meaning (e.g. if your child uses the wrong word and you are not sure what he means, then by all means suggest another word that might be more appropriate until the meaning becomes clear).

Another interesting study found that second language learners did no better at speaking with native language speakers than with other learners.[26] In other words, your child will make progress no matter whether you yourself speak the language fluently or not. It is not the quality that matters, it is the quantity. If nothing else, there is probably less pressure on children "to get it right from the start" with non-native speakers than there is with native speakers, and the less pressure there is, the more enjoyable it is for the child.

3. Strengthen the foundations for launching their own language genius. Aim to build up to 100 words (hot, cold, doll, up, down) as quickly as possible, and then build on those words to make phrases and finally sentences. Provide as many opportunities for simple conversation as you can - even if your child does not respond immediately, they will be learning. When they have learned enough words, surrounded by a rich environment, they will take off.

The key for strengthening the foundations is repetition. The advantage of starting young is that young children love repetition. They will quite happily watch the same DVD ten times in a week, play the same song over and over for hours, and ask you to read them the same book every day for months on end. Each medium provides a short story with a limited amount of words - the jigsaw pieces - and each repetition allows children to place the pieces together.

The rest of this guide focusses on how you as a parent might make the most of this approach, with suggestions of how to fine tune it depending on your own language strengths and weaknesses.

So, put aside your abc's and 123's for the moment: let's just get started with the rich world of language.

Chapter 3: Summary

How do children learn languages?

Babies and toddlers go through three main stages of language development:

- Learning to understand - through countless hours of listening
- Learning to speak - through countless hours of training their mouths to generate sound
- Becoming a language genius - through countless hours of speaking - and comparing that speech to everything they have absorbed before.

The implications of this for learning a second language is that you need to:

- Provide a rich environment from which they themselves can absorb the second language
- Listen to what they want to say - and provide them the words they need to get the results they want
- Shore up their foundation - using repetition as a key tool - so that they themselves can launch their own language genius.

In other words, put your Berlitz, Rosetta Stone and primary school textbooks back on the shelf, and start instead with what you think your child will want to hear. This is the real launchpad for language.

4. Getting started

Preparing yourself and your child for this new activity is not difficult, but it does require some decision-making, including:

- Choosing a language
- Choosing your role in the learning process
- Considering your goal
- Trying it out
- Setting a routine

Choosing a language

The first step in teaching your child a foreign language has to be to choose the language. There are many criteria you can use, including whether:

- you know the language already, at least a little
- you would like to learn it or learn it better
- you just enjoy the way it sounds
- you would like to visit the countries where it is spoken
- you have the opportunity to visit the countries where it is spoken
- the school your children will attend offers classes in the language, or even markets itself as a bilingual school.
- there is a good support network for that language in your community, e.g. teachers, nannies and neighbours who speak it, resources such as books, music etc.
- it is ultimately a useful language to learn (although this is a consideration, it should be a small one, as I have already

stressed it is the acquisition of a second language that is more important than the language itself).

There is no right choice, but I do recommend that you choose only one language, *if you are not a multilingual family already.* [27] For monolinguals, the investment in supporting bilingualism in a child can be substantial. For multilingual families, where parents or grandparents have access to different languages, it is actually sometimes easier: one person can speak one language to the children, a second the second, and so on.

My own theory is that the only way to guarantee any long-term success of your efforts is if you have an interest in it yourself (self-interest rules, I always say). If you have studied Italian on and off, listen to Italian opera, eat pasta regularly and visit Tuscany as often as your wallet allows, then that should indicate to you that Italian might be a good choice. If you are not enthusiastic, your children will know it, and you will fall off the language bandwagon at the first bump on the road. Enthusiasm is ten times more important than expertise in this area.

I looked into three languages when I considered which to teach my children: Spanish, a language I always wanted to learn but never even started; Dutch, the language of my heritage and the native language of most of my living relatives; and French, the language that I personally spoke the best.

With Spanish, I realised after some discussion that my husband did not have any interest in traveling there, and as I am a firm believer in some sort of immersion experience at some point, this significantly detracted from Spanish's appeal.

I also considered Dutch but then remembered how difficult it was to learn the language myself when everyone I met there spoke English nearly fluently. That is one country where language immersion programmes must fail spectacularly! Similarly, it is not as easy to find resources in the community as the language has a relatively small global footprint.

French had the following advantages: both my husband and I had a foundation knowledge of it; I enjoy visiting France and it is nearby enough to visit relatively easily; my boys' school had French classes from an early age; and I could see how exposing the language to my boys would help me at least maintain a little grasp of it, whereas otherwise the little I did know how to speak would easily become rusty.

Choosing your role

So far in this guide, we have focussed only on the children: why it is important for them to learn a language. What about you? What do you want to get out of this journey?

Every parent approaches this initiative from a different point in their own language development, and this will in part determine how you might approach language development with your children. Even if you have no interest in the language yourself you can still apply the methods in this book. Here is a simple framework to consider - try to decide which category you most closely fit into:

- **Minimal level of personal involvement:** You have no interest in learning the language you want your children to learn, and little time to allocate to it yourself. Yet you are still keen that your children pick up a second language.
- **Moderate level of personal involvement:** You would like to learn the language and plan to focus on it with your

children. You may also be interested in taking an adult language class to further your own abilities.

- **Significant level of personal involvement:** Through study or experience, you have learned the language before to at least an intermediate standard and hope to build on your knowledge through your activities with your children. If you are quite comfortable in the language, or just willing to "have a go", you may choose to lead some of the language activities yourself.

Let's take each level at a time.

Minimal. If you do not know a second language, and are not interested or motivated due to your own personal circumstances to make the effort yourself at this point in time, do not let that get in the way of your child learning a second language. You just have to engineer more opportunities with others: grandparents, nannies, babysitters, Saturday schools and whoever else you might find to take up the language guide for a few hours a week. It may take a little extra effort (and money) to find someone to be there consistently, but it is well worth it. One of my friends, a busy lawyer, arranged for au pairs to take care of her children when she worked. These au pairs were invariably from South America. Yet not once did it occur to my friend, her husband, their families, nor indeed the au pairs themselves, that these wonderful women, living in her own house, spending hours with her children, could help her children learn a new language. Why would our society be so blind to this marvellous opportunity!

Moderate. If you want to learn a new language, there is really no better motivation or way of practicing than with your children. They don't correct you (apart from your accent), or make you feel self-conscious. And they learn quickly too, so you have to keep up with them. They are the best study partners. And, learning a new language has an extra benefit: it encourages you to speak to your child. Literally, just speak. Apparently, babies benefit from a stream of speech directed at them. And yet I personally struggled with talking to my little boys when no one else was around. I was focussed on making meals, cleaning up, laundry, changing nappies. I found that if I instead focussed on practicing my French with them, I spoke more. I made up topics of conversation. It was as if it actually felt *less silly* to be speaking to someone who didn't speak back, if it were in another language. Well, it worked for me - maybe it will work for you too!

Significant. If you or a family member are bilingual, there are many issues you may be wrestling with that have given you doubts as to the best approach to teaching your child a second language. I am amazed at how many people I speak to who are bilingual but do not pass this on to their children. I have friends who are originally from Hong Kong, or India, or Italy, and are now living in the UK. Time and time again they tell me they don't do it, and they regret it, but they don't know how to square the circle of living in England, often with an English spouse, and their children in an English school, and still maintain speaking their own language. It somehow doesn't feel natural. In some ways, it isn't natural: it can be hard work, remembering what language to speak when, and putting extra pressure on yourself as a parent.

If you are a non-native English speaker now living in an English speaking country, you may feel impelled, as my mother was, to continue to improve your English skills rather than having to constantly revert to your native tongue. With that added baggage, you may wish your child to have the very best start in English, and feel that a second language would be an imposition. You may find it awkward or rude to speak your language with your child if your spouse and your friends do not understand.

Alongside all the pressure to NOT speak your language, you may have a deep desire (and/or significant pressure from your own family) to have your own child learn your native language, but feel like you don't have the time to do it because in your mind, you think you will have to do it all the time to make it worthwhile.

Remember that your children will never, ever reach adulthood and say that they wish you *hadn't* taught them a second language. Remember too that if you don't, they will most certainly blame you for *not* having taught them. So if you just want to avoid blame (heavens knows us parents get enough of it these days), teaching them a second language is the path to take.

To make matters more interesting, research has shown that children who are spoken to in the native language of their parents, no matter what language is spoken at school, will do better at school than children whose parents make the effort to match their child's schooling language even if it is not their own. Apparently, it is the richness of the language used, rather than the language itself, which contributes to the children's language development. Also, children with stronger ethnic identities, even if the identity is different from the identity of others at school, seem to develop greater confidence. Thus, celebrating difference seems to work better than hiding it.[28]

My mother never saw the point in teaching us her native language, Dutch. Yet we spent a great deal of our childhood holidays in Holland, where we had to speak with local children and family members who didn't speak English. By the end of my childhood I was a passive bilingual - I could barely speak Dutch (I was a shy child) but understood anything anyone said to me. This was enough of a foundation to motivate me to undertake a Dutch history subject for my undergraduate research project, and complete all the primary research in Dutch. While I have always berated my poor mother for not teaching us Dutch, nonetheless without any effort on her part she did enable us to gain a basic foothold in the language, for which I greatly benefited later in life.

The key here is to remember - for all parents - that learning a language is NOT an all or nothing option. Just like you don't have to spend every waking hour of every day counting with your child for them to learn maths, you don't have to spend every waking hour of every day speaking another language for them to benefit. You can choose to speak to your child as little or as much as you can fit in. You can choose to speak to your child in your native language only when other people are not around, for instance. You can choose to only speak to your child in that language when you are with family members who are fluent in that language. You can choose just to make it a part of the bedtime routine. I guarantee they will benefit even from the littlest amount.

The rest of the guide will try to provide pointers for parents on all parts of the spectrum, so if one idea does not match what you are trying to achieve, then do not give up - there will be other ideas that are much more suited to your style and abilities.

Considering the goal

The next step, well documented by Naomi Steiner in her book *7 Steps to Raising a Bilingual Child*, is to set an initial goal. In particular, Steiner recommends that parents "determine how proficient" they want their child to be. [29]

In this there is again a broad spectrum, and parents should consider how their goal matches their desired effort level. Some parents would love it if they could somehow enable their children to speak, read and write a second and even third language by the time they are eight years old, and are willing to enable their children to put in the time and effort required. Others would consider it a success if their children simply enjoyed being exposed to a new language and culture, without the need for measurable achievement.

Like learning maths, learning a foreign language is not an all-or-nothing option

There are perhaps four broad goals that can be pursued in language learning:

- **Foundation setting:** allowing your child to be exposed to the language and build a foundation for an interest and enjoyment in language learning later in life. This is no minor achievement. Children who have a basic foundation will have gained many of the benefits listed in Chapter 2: a basic enthusiasm for language which will get them past the initial hurdles when they start languages at school; an association of language learning with fun; a basic appreciation for other cultures and values; and even some of the academic advantages listed, depending on the length of time spent on language learning. A foundation in a foreign language is just as valuable as a foundation in maths or English: you don't need to aim to have your child achieve the Nobel Prize to know they have benefitted.

- **Passive bilingualism:** focussing primarily on building the ability to understand a language, with less emphasis on speaking, reading and writing. I am firmly of the belief that learning language passively, through speaking to them in one language and them responding back in English for instance, is still very useful. Children learn to understand, an excellent foundation to moving forward to speaking, if necessary at a later stage of development. In any human interaction abroad, you usually have time to look up a few words (where is the toilet?) but if you cannot understand the response you are probably in big trouble. A firm basis in comprehension is therefore a very useful tool to give your children indeed.

- **Active bilingualism:** focussing primarily on building the ability to converse in (understand and speak) the language. Most bilingual parents can easily aim for this goal, whereas non-bilinguals have to work a bit harder at this, or at a minimum have to find others to fill the role of providing regular conversation for their children in a second language. I strongly suggest you choose this goal if you would like an excellent excuse for frequent travel abroad!

- **Full bilingualism:** enabling your child to understand, speak, read and write. Full bilingualism is particularly tricky, in that the written part of many languages can vary significantly from the spoken word. Indeed, full written fluency even in a mother tongue takes most children the better part of their teenage years to master, so full written fluency in a second language would have to be a very long term goal for any parent.

I believe that unless you are both bilingual and confident in putting the time in, it is actually important not to set the bar too high initially. If you have any doubts about your commitment or the resources you have to support you, why not just set an initial goal to build a good language learning foundation for your child? If this goes well, then you can review your goals and set the bar higher for yourself and your child.

It is important to note at this stage that if you have more than one child your goals can and indeed may need to be different for each child. Remember that as they grow, each will have different learning styles; each will have different opportunities to converse and different support networks (teachers, friends etc); one's achievements may positively or negatively affect the other's motivations; inherent competition may cause one to rebel while the other excels.

Even the language resources you have available might be more attractive to one child than the other. As a parent, you will succeed in helping all your children children achieve their potential only if you treat each child individually. The key is to be aware of their differences, and do the best you can (within the resources you have available) to match with their individual needs. But don't beat yourself over the head with it, and if necessary let them achieve different levels of proficiency if it makes all of you happier as a result.

Trying it out

Once you have decided on your goal, Steiner recommends making a language learning action plan. Set out what you plan to do, when, and how; implement it; and then modify it as necessary.

Although I think this is excellent, as it makes you think through the physical steps required to achieving your goals, I also think for some people it can get in the way of action. When I started out, I was not sure how I was going to feel about speaking French, whether I could find the resources necessary, and how my children would react. I just wanted to dip my toe in the water, see how it would feel, and then take further incremental steps if and when we were ready. The lovely truth of language learning is that it is a lifelong pursuit, so there is no harm in starting slow and building up over a half dozen years if necessary.

So my key message is *just try it*! There are many ways to start out, as the listing in the next section suggests. Here are a few starting points:

- **Minimal Parent Involvement**: Outsource!!! Finding someone else to lead the charge can be a very effective way to help your child learn. Consider what childcare options you have that would involve a second language: hiring a nanny who speaks the language, enlisting a grandparent, to spend time with the children, or find a class or school that will be held in the language you choose. DVDs that play in both English and your chosen language are a good in-house option for preschool children.

- **Moderate Parent Involvement:** Consider setting up a class in which parents and children learn together. Also, take the time to undertake language-centered activities with your children, like watching DVDs, dancing to music, or surfing the net. You might be surprised at how hard you have to concentrate to keep up with your children. Children will be inspired to learn with you, and if they see you taking extra time to learn the language they may wish to make the extra effort themselves. Try involving them in helping you practice. Look up words that you know you might want to use with them on some activity the next day. Take their questions to your (or their) teacher to have them answered.

- **Significant Parent Involvement:** If you are bilingual already, or simply confident enough to do so, this could be as easy as just start speaking the language with your child. If the child is older and used to English, it may be important to introduce it gradually, over a period of weeks or even months. Start perhaps over breakfast. If it feels okay, continue building the time to converse, as and when it suits you and your children. Think about how to embed a little language conversation in everyday life. Consider how you all might benefit from a language immersion holiday. Try to tap into any language community in your area that might help reinforce your efforts.

Of course, you need to consider the age of your child when you start out.

Infants and young toddlers are passive language learners, as they do not yet have the full capacity for speech. As a result, you need to find things that they enjoy listening to and watching. For this age group, songs, books and at the later stages, short television programmes (in moderation) are ideal, as well as of course any kind of conversation.

From about two years old, children can participate in a class alongside you, again with the focus on songs and physical games. Then, by the age of three, your child should just be about ready to separate from you for a class, and will start to take more interest in games and toys.

From ages four to seven, most tools and topics - for instance internet games - will be accessible to your child. However, if you start your language learning with your child at this age, rather than earlier, you may have to introduce it much more slowly, to ensure that they do not feel it is a chore as much as a fun, shared activity.

Setting a routine

Once your child starts to enjoy these activities, and crucially, you find something that works for you, *then* you can move quickly onto the next step: *setting up rules* and *applying them consistently*. Rules are as important for you as they are for the child. Some examples of rules are:

- Exclusive rules: "DVDs should only be played in French."
- Rules based on time or place: "Friday is French DVD night."
- Rules based on parental roles: "Daddy plays DVDs in English but Mummy plays them in French."

I am a firm believer in setting clear, non-negotiable boundaries for children. With language learning there is a clear benefit: they know they cannot change the rule, so they simply go along with it.

The main goal should be to find a set of rules which both you and your child can stick to. The important thing is to get started, so it only has to work in the short term. Think in months or school terms if it helps. As the confidence of both you and your child grows, you may choose to extend your efforts. As your children grow, they may also challenge your rules (for instance, by learning to use the remote to change channels or languages). It is important to make any changes in a transparent way and to apply them consistently so that your child is not confused in any way, as this will undermine their efforts to learn a new language.

Chapter 4: Summary

To get started:

Choose a language by considering your own interests, your support network, and the school environment where your child will ultimately end up.

Choose your role, based on your own language experience and time available. If you have little time for languages yourself, don't deny your children the chance to develop one - just outsource!

Consider your goal, in terms of what you would like your children to achieve. Developing your child's ear for languages is just as useful a goal as aiming for full bilingualism.

Try it out by just taking on one activity at a time. It will seem less daunting if you can scale this hill just a small step at a time.

Set a routine that you can slowly add to. Make sure that you are consistent with your children and they will consistently surprise you with their learning.

5. The language bag of tricks: My top ten tools & techniques for language learning

You have chosen a language, you have decided how involved you will be. Now the trick is to create a language learning environment for your child. How will you do this? What will you use?

I have to say, I think that this is the most difficult question to answer, if you have never thought about teaching your child a language. What tools and techniques are at your disposal to have fun with your child learning a new language?

Yet, this is probably the most important area to consider (after choice of language, I guess). Firstly, because as I hopefully impressed on you before, creating a full language *environment*, where your child has access to lots of listening and interacting with the language, is crucial to the language learning process. Secondly, because children's interests and abilities change over time, so you will need a wide range of resources to keep them happy and engaged.

> **10 Tools & Techniques**
> 1. Television & DVDs
> 2. Music & audiobooks
> 3. Classes
> 4. Books & magazines
> 5. Internet & CD-Roms
> 6. Community resources
> 7. Holidays & immersion
> 8. Games & toys
> 9. Conversation
> 10. Reading & writing

Ten tools & techniques will be discussed in some detail in this chapter. Whilst each has its own advantages and challenges, I've attempted to rank them roughly in order of ease of use, from a monolinguist's point of view. For someone who does not speak the chosen language, the telly is the easiest option as it requires little or no language knowledge by the parent. Holding a conversation is much more difficult for the same person, and finally reading and writing is difficult even for many true bilinguals.

Some of these tools & techniques come at a financial cost. Conscious of the financial burden that raising children already imposes on parents, I have attempted to give some ideas of how to minimise cost.

What might help in choosing from this list of activities is to understand your own child's learning style, whether it be visual, aural or kinesthetic. I know that James is an incredibly visual child - he can sit and watch telly or look through picture books for hours. Scotty on the other hand is more aural - he loves listening to music and audio books. James learns through seeing, Scotty through hearing, and my efforts at helping them learn must reflect that (if I don't want to get too frustrated, anyhow). Having said that, the more of your child's senses you engage, the more of an impact you will have on their ability to learn.

One word of warning: what you don't see on this list is any specific language programme, e.g. Berlitz, Rosetta Stone, Muzzy etc. These programmes usually involve a textbook, activity book, CD and/or DVD. In my early attempts to find something for my children to learn, I did purchase one or two language programmes specifically geared for kids. Unfortunately, what I didn't realise until I had handed over my precious cash was that many of these are geared for older (10+) children rather than young children. The others are fairly limited in their language use. I have dutifully stashed them away for the future, but frankly I think that with a little effort and lots of fun my boys will be far ahead of these beginner guides by the time they reach the age they can use them.

Instead, read below to see the hundreds of resources that are available, under your very nose, right now. You will be astonished at what you can easily do to transform your child's environment to one suited for learning a second language, without resorting to an "expert" language programme to guide you.

Television & DVDs

As a parent, we are bombarded by advice NOT to let our children watch television. At the same time, the so-called "Living Room Babysitter" is a temptation to which most parents succumb. My solution: let them watch (in moderation) - in French! I get peace and quiet to get on with my chores, they enjoy watching tv - and learn another language.

There is a certain amount of research out there that suggests that children in fact cannot learn a language from the telly. To a certain extent, this is true. A one-way monologue in Urdu is not going to get your children to speak Urdu fluently. Children do need a minimum level of interaction - conversation directed to them at a level they can understand during which, even if they do not speak, they must react to words spoken to them - to gain proficiency in a language.

On the other hand, everyone who has tried to learn a language knows that half the battle in having a conversation is not speaking - it is understanding what the other person is saying. Today's television programmes aimed at young children provide significant advantages over other forms of passive learning in that they provide short repetitive sentences tied to easily understood visual clues as to what is being said, which aids comprehension tremendously. When Dora the Explorer says *"est-ce que tu vois le pic enneigé"*, and a snowy mountain comes into view, and then she says *"le pic enneigé"* three more times while pointing to it, then pretty soon your children will understand what a *"pic enneigé"* is. Indeed, when we recently went to France on a ski holiday, my son James pointed to the first snow-capped mountain he saw and said *"un pic enneigé"* three times - until I finally understood what he was saying...

I am a big fan of DVDs. The reason for this is not only do you avoid your children being constantly bombarded with advertisements (a real bonus), but the fact that as a parent I have total control. I can pick the DVD programme that suits the time available, our mood and the current interests of the day. They are relatively cheap, especially as the children really do like to watch them over, and over, and over, and over.

For language learning, repetition is a wonderful thing. I remember once, when I was living in France, going to see the film *Cyrano de Bergerac*. At first, I couldn't understand much of what was going on; just enough, in fact, to make me fall in love with the film. I ended up seeing it 4 more times over the course of 4 weeks. Every time I saw it, I understood more and more of the dialogue. Finally, by the end, I understood more or less all of it. Your children benefit from rewatching DVDs just as much, especially if you spend the first or second time watching it with them and helping to translate, or playing it in English and your chosen language alternately. That way, they will understand it enough to enjoy it, and afterwards they can continue to pick up words with every viewing.

> *When your children are watching DVDs in another language, keep your ears open for snippets of language words and phrases - before and after. It's fun to hear! For instance, Scotty and James were chasing each other around one day and Scotty ran into the kitchen shouting "Au secours, a l'aide, au secours!" (help, rescue me, help!) with a big grin on his face. James then ran in saying "Scooby Dooby Doo!"*

Some basic tips to using your television wisely:

- Stock up on DVDs. DVDs often come in multiple languages, and can be purchased second-hand quite cheaply over the internet, or borrowed from the library. Popular cartoons such as Dora the Explorer and Scooby Doo come in most modern European languages. Check the back of any DVD box to see what languages are available. For younger children, play the DVD in English first and then switch to your chosen language, or switch between the two. (James has caught on to the fact that my husband can't figure out how to switch DVDs into French. If James wants a DVD played in English he will ask his Dad to put it on. My counterattack has been to purchase DVDs direct from Amazon.fr, where the default language is French.) For older children, you can put the DVD on in your chosen language and put the English subtitles on to assist in comprehension. This of course has the advantage of improving their English reading skills. (One note of caution is you must ensure that the DVDs you purchase are in the right format for your region: Region 1 for USA, Region 2 for Europe, etc. Multi-regional DVD players are available for purchase as well but they are not usually sold as standard).

- Subscribe to satellite television. If you choose to do this, make sure that your satellite provider can access television programming from the country of your choice, and ensure that the installer can demonstrate that those channels are indeed available. This can help when your stock of DVDs is low, or the language you have chosen for your child is not readily available on DVDs, and it provides a much wider range of child-centered programming. Recording native language programmes is advisable as you can replay the best ones to your child over and over again, which aids learning considerably.

- Access foreign television via the internet. Many shows are not only available to view but also to download, making it easier to find programmes, download them on a recordable DVD and play them over and over (and over and over and over).

- Use portable DVD players for long journeys in the car, train or plane - children will watch almost anything in that environment. This also provides a great opportunity to introduce DVDs that children have otherwise resisted (even though you know they would enjoy them).

- Where possible, watch the programmes with them. If necessary, have a dictionary at hand and you might be able to translate a few tricky words as well as check their understanding from time to time. They enjoy the programme more when you are there, which heightens their enjoyment generally of the language experience.

Although some children will watch anything that flickers on television (my eldest being a prime example), others are much more choosy. It is of course vital to find something that will hold your child's interests. After that however, there are some criteria you may want to consider in choosing television programmes for your child:

- **Age of your child.** For children under two, it is not recommended that they watch any television. If you want to let them watch something, it is best to watch short programmes (20 minutes or less) and watch it with them, so it remains an interactive experience. For children over two, only gradually increase the amount of time that they are exposed to screens. The maximum recommended amount of screen time (television, games and internet) is two hours' average use per day.

- **Length.** Cartoons and other children's programmes made for television tend to be 10-20 minutes in length, whilst films originally made for the cinema can be up to two hours. A 20-minute programme is more likely to hold the attention of a small child, and can be more easily played repeatedly (by you or the television provider), both of which are important for language learning.

- **Learning-centred programmes**. Many recent programmes created for younger children are geared towards learning: Dora the Explorer, Blues' Clues, and Teletubbies being prime examples. These programmes are highly repetitive both in terms of script and in terms of language use, and many make attempts at luring children to interact by yelling out answers or copying physically the movements on the screen. As such, they lend themselves superbly to translation into your chosen language. I firmly believe both my boys learned a large amount of French vocabulary simply through watching Dora & Diego.

- **Entertainment-centred programmes**. Programmes such as Scooby-Doo, Wacky Races, Bugs Bunny and Cinderella are fun for children to watch in whatever language, as the visual antics are well-choreographed and thus do not require language to be amusing. Nonetheless they often seemed to be accompanied by strong accents, some adult humour and fast-paced dialogue. These programmes are therefore less useful for beginners but once a minimum level of vocabulary is achieved, they can play a big part in exposing your child to the language - not least because they love watching them.

- **Programmes** can be usefully transformed into themes or conversation pieces. Taking the time after a programme to discuss it, in your chosen language, for even five minutes, will give you and your child a chance to practise speaking and using the language that you have just heard.

- For older children, subtitles are a terrific learning tool. On visiting my younger cousins in Holland when I was 12, I noticed for the first time how much English they knew, despite not having started learning it at school. Then I sat down to watch the Smurfs with them one day, and was amazed to see that all the cartoons were played in English with Dutch subtitles. They had literally learned all their English language skills through cartoons.

Music & audiobooks

Music has a central role to play in any child's learning process, as it seems to engage children easily and enjoyably. Bernadette Tynan, author of *Make Your Child Brilliant*, states that "songs are irresistible to the brain and how memory works because they activate both the left and right hemispheres of the brain, stimulating them to work together."[30] Her premise is that making connections between the different sides of the brain - one being the language centre, and the other being the centre of creativity - will embed knowledge much more quickly. I don't know about you, but I'm always amazed at what songs I end up singing under my breath while doing my daily chores - how did they get into my brain so quickly?

Learning songs is an excellent way to gain vocabulary in another language as songs often repeat specific words and phrases. And of course, there is usually a superb supply of children-centred songs in any given language, if you can access them.

Similarly, nursery rhymes, poems and fairy tales have great appeal for children. They are rhythmic, and often play on the specific language sounds you would like your children to be able to pick up and repeat correctly.

My two boys have really taken to French nursery rhymes and songs. Initially I played one CD after another in the car, each for perhaps at least a month at a time. They listened to them intently, and sang a little where they could. Recently I put them back in the car and was amazed at how they seemed to pick up the words much more quickly and easily, and enjoyed them even more as a result. That magic tool - repetition - seemed to work again in the area of music and songs. Even if they don't take to a song initially, never throw the CD away - there will come a time that they will want to hear it again and again and again, and learn from it as a result. An even stronger bond with the music can be made if there is an accompanying book, as this will help with the vocabulary, and the pictures will engage the children in the story line.

Specialist websites such as www.little-linguist.co.uk and http://www.linguatots.com provide an excellent source of music. As with books, they come in various guises:

- **Language learning songs**. These songs have been put together with language learning in mind, and therefore focus on certain sets of vocabulary such as days of the week or numbers. These products provide access to a good set of vocabulary however the tunes may not always be as engaging as traditional songs (unless they have used traditional songs and changed the words).

- **Bilingual songs.** These have the strengths and weaknesses as above, as they are written for the same purpose. They have the additional advantage of providing the child (and parent) with ongoing translation, so that they can understand what the song is trying to say. The best versions of these will manage to sing only a few words in one language and then the same words in another - say 3 words in French and then the 3 words in English. When the words are translated by verse, the meaning of the whole song can be understood but it is difficult for the child to grasp the meaning of particular words.

- **Traditional songs and rhymes.** These are engaging as they have stood the test of time. The music is strong and the story lines within the songs are also interesting and fun. Nevertheless, the vocabulary is not always as relevant (for instance, there are often older words that are not in use now), and of course a translation is needed to help the children understand what they are singing. I admit that my children and I most enjoy these types of songs, however I have to look up a lot of words in the dictionary.

- **Audiobooks.** I have found that well-known stories, such as fairy tales, are excellent for engaging the children, for instance in the car, as the tales are internally repetitive and recognisable. Scott particularly likes *The Gingerbread Man* at the moment, a story that is particularly repetitive and attractive to happily mischievous and somewhat hungry children.

No particular category of these is better than the other - it is often just a case of hit or miss in terms of what your children enjoy listening to. It may also be a question of what to play at what time: traditional songs and rhymes can be played in the kitchen when doing arts & crafts (interrupted every now and then for a dance or two), whereas bilingual songs could be played in the car. Your interaction with the song and with the children - through dance, or making fun of the words - will make the songs more enjoyable for the children - and the more enjoyment, the more learning.

All audio options are significantly enhanced by the inclusion of a book to go alongside. Younger children's language development is reinforced by pictures that go along with the songs and stories, and older children benefit from the written words. If possible, ensure that what you buy comes with some sort of supporting written material.

On the cost-side, audio material can be more expensive than DVDs as it is more difficult to find such products second-hand and more difficult to choose something that you think the children will like. It is possible to tune in directly - and for free - to native language sources through digital radio, internet radio and long wave, although I suspect it is more relevant to older children as child-centered radio broadcasts are relatively rare.

Classes & playgroups

While the other tools and techniques suggested here are superb for providing your children with a rich language environment, classes can be an invaluable part of the learning process, especially if you yourself are not a native speaker of the language. The reason for this is **not** because young children need to focus on grammatical rules, or be taught sentence structures, or endlessly repeat vocabulary lists. It is simply because a good teacher can encourage conversation, in the most natural way possible, and use that conversation to help children *notice* when the way they speak does not match the spoken language. This is particularly

true when any mistakes they make do not affect the meaning of the conversation.

Let me give you a simple example. Children who speak French have the daunting task of learning the gender of each and every object they wish to speak about. A tree is **un** *arbre* but a chair is **une** *chaise*. Now, a good teacher will emphasise the genders of words and in a non-intrusive way help the child notice that it is **un** *arbre*, hopefully without interrupting the flow of conversation in the class. A class with a well-chosen instructor therefore helps your child achieve a higher level of fluency.

If you think that your child would benefit in this way from a class, the next step is to find one - or create one. One option is simply to wait: many primary schools offer classes in your chosen language from an early age; some forward-thinking nurseries even offer a French or Spanish "class" which may focus on songs or nursery rhymes, colours and numbers. This may be one of your selection criteria for the school or indeed, vice versa, for the language you choose to teach your child.

As with most classes, children only really start learning independently from the age of three years. Earlier than that, you or another adult will have to be intimately involved in the class and the benefits will depend very much on your child's attention span. On the other hand, early involvement in classes, especially if they are fun and involve the children's friends, will signal to children that language learning is an enjoyable experience rather than an extra burden or chore. If you wish to supplement anything that is offered in school, you have several options for younger children:

- If nothing is offered at school or nursery, there is no harm in suggesting to the school that it offers classes, or at a minimum set up a lunchtime or after school class.
- Approach a recognized programme such as La Jolie Ronde that may have classes in your area (even if they don't, they

might be encouraged to set one up if you can muster enough interest among your friends)

- Approach the local language school to see if they have classes geared towards children. Some even offer family classes to encourage the whole family to take part.
- Find the relevant country association to see if they run classes. Saturday classes are a popular option for large foreign language communities.
- Set up your own class at home.

Prices can range from £3 ($4) per hour per child upwards, depending on the number of children participating, the qualifications of the teacher and any franchise fees. Another option is to see if your community has a family with children of a similar age to yours who are native speakers of your chosen language, where the mother or father might be willing to help out with a home-run class.

If you wish to set up your own class at home, contact your local nursery, primary school, language school or foreign language community for the

A close friend who has children the same age as mine was the one who suggested starting up a class at home. I found a French teacher through the local primary school. We then invited our whole mummy/toddler group to join in and hold classes once a week. We split the fees, which are fairly inexpensive as we don't have to pay for a venue. We just started rotating houses, primarily to keep the kids on their toes and the resultant housekeeping to a minimum!

details of language teachers who might be interested in private teaching. Invite your children's friends to join in - the more they see it as a fun, inter-active ses-sion, the more they will enjoy it. But don't exceed six pupils per teacher if at all possible. If you are hosting a class at home, why not propose to rotate houses? It can make it more fun for the children and less stressful for the parents.

Here are a few hints and tips for home classes:

- As with any type of class, be aware that from time to time children will not be in the mood to learn. Depending on when the class is scheduled, children might be tired or hungry. They might have recently undergone some change: a new nursery, or a friend leaving. Any of this might affect their ability to concentrate, and the teacher needs to be sensitive to this and be able to change to something more appropriate to the child's attention span if necessary.

- If there are bilingual children in the class, or a great variation of abilities in the class, it is important to structure lessons in a way that allows the more advanced children to learn - indeed to shine - without getting in the way of the learning of the less advanced children. Consider creating a teacher's helper role and advising those children in advance of any particular activity what their role is, so that they know not to overshadow the others.

- Children love to be rewarded for their efforts and the simplest of these is a sticker at the end of class to show that they have participated. Reward charts, filled in over a term, can help the children focus, and end-of-term certificates help show both the children and the parents what has been achieved. In the best of all possible worlds, the process of listing out what the children are going to learn, learning it, and then presenting them with a certificate listing their achievements, can be a great motivator.

- It goes without saying that as in any situation where the teacher may gain the trust of your child, and may be left alone with your child, it is better to ensure that the relevant criminal record checks have been run. This can be organised fairly easily through your local authority.

Some schools offer a language as part of the standard curriculum already at Reception. Nevertheless, it might be worthwhile investing some time into making the language more than just another course: to find ways to make it a fun and regular part of their day or week.

Playgroups are another option if one or more parents are willing to engage the children (and each other) in your chosen language. The emphasis ideally should be on a specific hobby or simply playtime, with the language as the backdrop, to increase the enjoyment, relax the children and allow the language to be learned through play rather than rote.

After several years of practice at home, my two boys started a French bilingual school on Saturday mornings. The teachers were aware that all the children had already had a full week of classes in English school so the emphasis was on fun and games, with an underlying focus on the French national curriculum. The boys enjoyed playing with new friends and within only one month I could hear the benefits of two and a half hours full immersion in the boys' speech.

> ### *Monique Barb's advice on teaching small children*
>
> *"Small children ask questions all the time; they respond to meaning even if they do not understand individual words; their understanding comes not only from explanation, but also from what they see and hear, and most of all from what they have the chance to touch, feel and interact with; they generally display an enthusiasm for learning and curiosity about the world around them; they need individual attention and approval from the teacher; they are developing the sense of fairness and they begin to question the teacher's decisions; ...they have a limited attention span; they get bored easily if the activity is not interesting or engaging. Teachers teaching at this level need special skills, which are completely different from those needed elsewhere in the education system.*[31]

Something as simple as inviting friends around to play against each other on their Nin-tendo Wii (turned on in French), with a French speaking player there as a facilitator to encourage everyone to speak in French. Perhaps an Italian person you know is happy to have a run a face and nail painting session for a number of girls once a week, and with the only requirement for the girls to attempt to speak some Italian. How about a toddler baking class? Or a lego building session?

The multi-sensory environment offered by these types of activities is fabulous for improving the ability to learn. And let's face it - we do not learn our mother tongue by rote learning - we learn it through our daily lives - our games and activities and hobbies - why should we learn another language differently?

One final option to consider - if it is available - is immersion schooling. This is where your child is sent to a school where the language of instruction - the language used by the teachers and expected in the classroom - is in your chosen language. This of course will be the norm if your home language is different from the language of the country you live in. But even if it is not, there are some specialist schools that offer a different or even multi-language environment. Ac-cording to research, im-mersion schooling can be fantastic for your child. It multiplies exponentially the amount of time your child is exposed to the chosen lang-uage. It makes com-munication real and nec-essary. And your child will move on quickly from colours and numbers to much more interesting subjects to engage his imagination.

On a more cautionary note, children who undertake this type of schooling will initially (at a minimum for the first year) need a significant amount of extra support. They may find it daunting to try to speak a new language and fulfil the require-ments set by the teacher. They will be more tired than usual because their brains will be working overtime to make sense of everything they hear. Without extra support, either provided by the school or at home, the experience might actually be demotivating for the child.

A middle option is a Saturday school, where children spend at least half a day at a language school usually not only learning the language but also keeping up with parts of the curriculum that are usually offered in the country where the language is spoken. These can be found in most cities where there is a large foreign language community.

Books & magazines

Studies have shown that children pick up a significant amount of their vocabulary through books - being read to, and reading themselves. A study by Janet Patterson in 2002 found that "the size of [children's] vocabularies in each language could be predicted by how often they were read to in each language. In fact, the frequency with which children were read to in a foreign language had even more of an impact than the total exposure they had to the language." [32]

A book, like a DVD or song, is enjoyed most by children in repetition. This has so many advantages for the parent keen on teaching their child a second language. Firstly, because initially you don't actually need that many. Secondly, because you don't actually need to learn much vocabulary - just enough to read the book! Thirdly, because it provides a lovely quiet time with your child that will increase both of your language enjoyment.

Crucially, books in your chosen language are easier to come by than you would think.

There again are several types of books available:

- **Vocabulary books.** Usborne's series "First Hundred Words" or "First Thousand Words" are a great example. These books simply set out to teach loads of vocabulary, in a simple and attractive format. They usually come with lots of add-ons, such as sticker books, DVDs and CDs, even cuddly dolls. These can be particularly helpful if you yourself are not confident in your vocabulary - often they even come with pronunciation guides. Great word games can be played with these books, such as pointing to pictures and intentionally saying the wrong word - for instance pointing to a tree and saying that it is a table - kids love catching you out. The major drawback of these books is that they rarely include full sentences, so children do not learn verbs, adjectives or sentence structures, nor do they have true stories which the children can fully enjoy.

- **Bilingual books**. These are books that include the story in both English and your chosen language. This is great as you can read the story in English so that they are familiar with it, and then change to the other language. For children who are already reading in English, the English story line can work as "subtitles" for when you are reading the story in the other language. Unfortunately, the majority of books published in this format are marketed for the education establishment and therefore lack some of the story telling pizzazz of the best children's books.

- **Foreign language books.** There are two kinds of these books: books that were originally in English and have been translated and books that have been written originally in your chosen language. One great example of the first kind is the "Spot the Dog" series, by Eric Hill: they have a simple storyline, opening flaps and excellent illustrations which make them very appealing in any language.

- **Magazines.** It is often possible to subscribe to children's magazines in a foreign language. The costs are high in comparison to the content but there is a certain excitement for children in having a magazine delivered directly to the door with their name on it!

- **Electronic books.** Leapfrog's brand of electronic books, Leapster, has a number of titles which are available in French or other languages, including Dora & Spongebob.

For pre-reading children, if you are confident enough or simply have access to a good dictionary, you can just use English language picture books and do the translation yourself. This is of course easiest when there is very little or repetitive text: and let's face it, many enjoyable picture books do fit that description. Jez Alborough books, for instance, are typically at least a dozen pages long and only have one or two words in them.

Stories and any kind of storytelling are in fact a much more natural way for children to pick up words than vocabulary lists. The stories provide the framework on which your children's brains can store the words they learn. They provide a context that makes the words meaningful to them. Words without such context are really little use to children (or adults). I would banish those vocabulary lists altogether, apart from the fact that my children do love the stickers and colouring that often goes with vocabulary books, and these then provide a little fun to go along with the learning process.

The easiest way to purchase foreign language books (and indeed most other language resources) is online, where there are again two main options: using a specialist retailer, such as www.little-linguist.com, which stocks most of these types of books, or similarly trying an generalist international retailer, such as Amazon. Another option is directly ordering on a native language website, such as (in my case) www.amazon.fr.

But before opening your very own www.amazon.fr account, and potentially spending your monthly salary on just a handful of books, check out the local library. In many cities there is a small foreign language book section right in the children's library, and if not children's books can be obtained via the loan system. When we had run out of interesting foreign language books in our library I just asked if they could borrow any ten picture books from another. In a week I had all of these at home to share with my children.

Also, when you are on holiday in the country of your choice, don't forget to make time to purchase books and magazines before you return home. We found some lovely Dora and Diego books in French which were inexpensive and instantly recognisable for the children. I have left them in our book box downstairs and the children will often choose them for their bedtime story - out of a selection of both English and French books. Let's not forget that for some children, reading Dora books is lots of fun - no matter what the language.

Internet & CD-Roms

My eyes were opened to this possibility again through a friend, whose children play on a website called www.lcfclubs.com. This is a subscription service which offers games, songs, rhymes and other activities for children, in various languages. My two are hooked on it and the littlest one loves the songs in particular, and has as a result been heard quite frequently rapping in French.

The easiest suitable websites to find are those set up by broadcasting companies that offer children's programmes, such as the BBC, but it is important to look further afield. The equivalent of *Cheebies* and *Nick Jr* can be found in many countries, allowing parents to find children's sites that are for native language speakers. In my own search I've found excellent French and French Canadian websites which all cater to French-speaking children.

Youtube also has an amazing selection of videos to watch: simply type in "learn French" or "learn Mandarin" in the Youtube search engine and a whole host of potential videos pop up. It is very important of course to watch these yourself before showing them to your children, to make sure it is suitable for their viewing.

For younger children without any reading skills, websites that include a vocal element will be most useful. For instance, many children's sites offer memory/matching games, however some of them will match written words to pictures, whereas others will just have the pictures but will repeat the name of the picture every time it is clicked on. The vocal element is thus crucial to making the site useful for pre-reading children, at least if they are playing on the site independently. Just don't forget to ensure your computer's speakers are turned on...

Obviously, children need to be closely monitored when using the internet, and any sites promoting any kind of two-way conversation particularly scrutinised. Used carefully, however the internet provides unparalleled opportunities for valuable exchanges across continents.

Good sites have recommendations for children immediately on entering the site to ensure that they do not share any contact details with others, and ask children to involve their parents in their conversations.

There are a number of CD-Roms available which are geared towards language learning for younger children. The advantage over internet sites is that many of these allow your children to follow a particular programme rather than just dipping in and out of various games and stories offered by websites. The disadvantage is that of course there is a cost. In my experience, it is not necessarily true that the higher the cost, the better the CD-Rom. Usually, it is just a question of target markets: CD-Roms targeted for use in schools tend to be much more expensive than those for home use.

On a practical note, many CD-Roms can be played in multiple languages, so when searching for appropriate products it may be necessary to search using the generic word "language" rather than "French" or whatever your chosen language may be. Also, as with all software purchases, be aware of the technical specifications: for instance, many CD-Roms will only play on PCs but not on Apple computers.

Sometimes schools will be licensed to use particular software and/or sites which they may be able to make available to you as well, depending on the license agreement. In my experience, there is no harm in asking about the resources a school has and how you might benefit.

It is worth noting that you can also purchase language learning "apps" for the iPhone and other smartphones. I haven't yet found one suitable for children but it is probably worth looking for as they are usually cheap, accessible and most children associate such apps with fun and games, a great starting point for learning.

Community-based resources

In many larger cities, and certainly those of one million or more residents, there are a multitude of pockets of foreign cultures. New York may have Chinatown and Little Italy more or less on the map, but many other cities have similar geographical areas if you know where to look for them. In them, restaurants, shops and cafes might have owners and staff who speak the language you are introducing to your child. Visit them and start conversations, with your child in tow. If it isn't busy, the staff are likely to encourage your efforts and your child will notice and may even be outgoing enough to take part. If it works out, make it a regular outing.

Other cities have thriving cultural associations not based on geography but on social affiliation. A friend of mine takes her daughter to regular outings by the local Spanish club, so that she can play with other children who speak, or are learning, Spanish. A local French association found it had enough parents of small children to set up a regular play date, held in French.

For people less confident with their conversation skills, it is still worth looking up local associations to attend celebrations and festivals, where the languages will probably be mixed but you and your children can appreciate some of the cultural aspects of the language you are learning.

Local associations are usually easy to find on the internet; an alternative is to contact the nearest embassy or consulate for information on social networks. Teachers at local language schools (for adults as well as for children) might also be able to provide information on cultural associations.

Holidays & immersion

Ah, I love holidays. I love planning holidays. And now, I love planning holidays with a language element to them. Trickier, but very rewarding!

I admit that part of my motivation in helping my boys learn French is that it forces me - twist my arm - to go abroad, to a French speaking country, as often as possible. (My current aim is at least once a year, which we are just about achieving.) In my view, the purpose of learning a language is to use it, and using it means being in the country on the ground talking to people who speak it as their first language.

Children need to see that people really do use the language every day.

Another important role of holidays is getting the children excited and involved in the experience. If you spend time in advance planning the holiday and making it clear that they will be expected to speak the language from time to time (or all the time) then they will be more mentally prepared. You can even do the planning in your chosen language, to get them used to it.

There are three types of holidays that can be counted as assisting your child to learn another language, on a continuum from easy-going to, well, geeky:

- **Tourist holidays.** Pick a country where the language is spoken: not just the country where the language originated, but anywhere it is used. For us, France is closest, but other destinations include exciting places such as Guadeloupe, Quebec, North Africa and Mauritius. We recently went to Honfleur in Normandy for a long weekend and the children quickly learned the words such as "*la plage*" (beach), "*arrete, voitures!*" (stop, cars!), "*merci*", etc. In these types of holidays, the onus is on you to speak with them, and to translate. Don't worry if you aren't a linguist. Look up a few useful words and use them frequently. Do be aware that your little attempts to get them to interact (for instance, order a glass of milk at a restaurant) might be thwarted by less-than-patient locals, just as often as they might be rewarded by encouraging smiles. These holidays are a lovely, gentle way to make the children aware that indeed the language you have been drip-feeding them at home actually is spoken by real people all the time. However it may not get your children much closer to speaking themselves.

- **Child-centered holidays**. Again, pick a country where the chosen language is spoken, and then pick a resort or package where the children are involved in activities all day long, with other children. Ski and beach holidays lend themselves well to this. The key is to choose a holiday provider that markets itself either primarily or better still exclusively to native language speakers. That way, all the activities will be provided in the native language, and most of the other holiday-makers, including the children, will be native language speakers. Inevitably, this creates the problem that you might have to do your research in that language, book the holiday in that language and cope yourself in that language. A learning experience for everyone!

- **Language-centered holidays**. These are holidays in which a language school of some sort is the base. Some language schools even offer family packages which include language tuition in the morning, followed by activities or excursions in the afternoon. Other schools may simply have different course levels. I have just recently managed to find a language immersion course at a language school in France geared to families with young children, but they are few and far between so there is certainly a gap in the market that someone somewhere should fill.

Of course, these are all on a continuum and you might find a perfectly good tourist holiday in which your children make excellent progress in speaking, simply because the friends they make are native language speakers. If we could guarantee that outcome up front, we would certainly save a lot of money and stress!

When on holiday, it might be necessary to revise your normal rules to suit your new environ-ment. A friend of mine insists that if her boys want to enjoy a drink or snack abroad, they must order it themselves. Even just ordering ice cream can be a great vocabulary builder, especially in France or Italy where the average ice cream stand has dozens of flavours and sizes to choose from. Yum, yum, yum....

We have now been (a big splurge, but worth it!) to an all-inclusive ski resort in France marketed only to French people. The children attended kids' clubs and ski lessons during the day, in a French-only envir-onment, while we skied. To our surprise, the children seemed to have no hesitation going to the clubs, and enjoyed the little interactions they could manage in the native language. In the end, they did seem to have a great time and want to know when they can go back.

The time element is another one to consider with holidays. Of course, the longer that you can be immersed in a foreign language environment the better. One week is just a taster; two weeks is the minimum to gaining some real progress; but in just four weeks you can turn a monolingual child into a bilingual chatterbox. In all these scenarios, the weeks and months that go by after a holiday will start to erode any progress, so ideally you need to find ways to build on the newly learned skills before you even cross the border back home.

Immersion experiences - staying in a country for more than just a holiday - are easier to organise nowadays than ever before. Firstly, because work is rather more flexible and international than in the past, with people being able to work from home, hot-desking at any company office, or hopping on ever more frequent cheap flights to "commute";

but also because more people speak English abroad than ever before, as there are more native English speakers abroad in many popular places.

In France alone, much of Normandy, the Alps and the Mediterranean coastline are overrun with expatriate English families, seeking a different lifestyle from their homeland. Many people have holiday homes across the continent that they only use for holidays, but could easily be used for a six or twelve month stay abroad if planned carefully. As a result, even if you are less than confident in a foreign language, you can still get by in such places without much strain, whilst your children attend the local school. Banking, home buying and letting and transport can all be undertaken with the help of English speaking mediators, making the transition unbelievably simple. Putting aside the amazing cultural and linguistic opportunities that immersion experiences affords both you and your children, consider the options for exploring other interests: skiing in the Alps, surfing in Portugal, biking in Holland, ruins exploration in Italy. The opportunities for happily bribing your child to learn the language multiply one thousand-fold. If your work and family situation are such that this is even a remote possibility, I suggest considering in strongly. If you pick the right destination, no doubt you won't have a chance to become homesick for all the visitors you will have!

Games & toys

Technology has made games and toys an excellent (and may I say, rather sneaky) way to help children learn a language. Many electronic games these days have the option to change the default language. This is particularly useful once your children have started to read, as the written instructions and game features will be in the chosen language. If your child is desperate for a Nintendo Wii or DS, make them a deal: if you buy it, they play it only in your chosen language. Better still, you can purchase "games" for these consoles which are geared specifically towards helping your child speak your chosen language.

Special language toys are also available now that technology has made it easy. Jolie, a French-language doll, speaks a few nice French phrases and is just one of many Language Little dolls. Certain toys can be switched to other languages, such as the Leap Frog Fridge Phonics and Fridge Farm collections. These type of toys have very limited vocabulary benefits, but are excellent as launchpads for conversation. For instance, you can pretend Jolie (see picture) is real and ask her questions, which your child will want to answer.

For traditionalists, technology-free games offer fabulous possibilities as well, as long as you do your homework. It is amazingly easy to turn several common board games into language learning opportunities. Here is a small selection of some options:

- **Bingo**. All you and your children need to know is your numbers, or whatever pictures might be shown on a picture bingo game.

- **Picture Lotto/Memory/Snap/Pick a Pair**. Just look up what each of the pictures on the cards is, and then say them when your child is turning the cards over. Make it a rule to say the name of what is on the card in the foreign language before they can earn any pairs. These games have an amazing ability to push your children to recall words and speak them quickly and clearly.

- **Guess Who?** Why not learn how to describe the faces in your chosen language and teach your kids?

It is also possible to purchase specialist language learning games. For instance, I purchased a version of Bingo in French in which you play a CD which calls out the words in French. Others specially made for language learning include Monopoly Junior and Spell Time.

Similarly, it is possible to purchase popular board games in their original language from an international retailer such as Amazon. This can have the advantage of helping to acquire cultural knowledge as well as vocabulary.

Even without the assistance of physical games, fun can easily be had with a little language preparation. How about a weekly treasure hunt, where the children can only claim the prize if they name all their treasures in the right language. Hide and seek with teddies is great for even the youngest toddlers: a fun way to learn to count and understand directions. Even if you are using only a handful of words or phrases, you are making the connection between language and fun. And that is really, in the end, what it is all about.

Conversation

No doubt one of the best ways to help your child speak a foreign language is to speak it with them. This is the area in which parents who are already bilingual have a major advantage over beginners. For us mere mortals, there is only one requirement when it comes to holding a conversation with your child: at a minimum, stay one step ahead of them. This does not mean knowing every bit of vocabulary.

My son once asked me how to say "the round track that turns the train" in French - well, I didn't even know how to say them in English. (Now I know - it's a turntable - I think. I still don't know what it is in French). It is okay to say "I don't know", but better if you have a dictionary at hand. I keep one in a drawer in the kitchen.

One step ahead means just knowing a few extra phrases and vocabulary words, so as to play conversation games. Simple questions can give entertainment over an entire meal, such as "Do you like _____?" "No, I don't like _____." Or simply point to something and say "What is this - *qu'est-ce que c'est?*" Make sure you know the answer! Or turn this on its head: for instance, point to a chair and say "this is a banana". Kids think this is hilarious and will want to correct you as soon as possible!

My children enjoy a few word games that we have adapted for use in a second language. One is the traditional "I spy" which we play in the car. This makes it pretty easy to limit the vocabulary to words we all know (road, sky, grass, trees, cars, etc). Another one is a game we made up called "how do you say" (*comment dit-on*, in French) which works on the same principle. The first person picks a word in either English or French and says *comment dit-on* "dog" and the first person to say *"le chien"* gets to have a turn. Another game that is easily played out and about is "I went to the zoo & I saw..." where each person has to add an animal and remember each animal that everyone else has already mentioned. We often do this when we have to wait somewhere for a short while, for instance in a restaurant, or in the post office queue.

Another tack, which can be quite useful if you are relatively comfortable in the language, is to set a time of day, or a particular place, to speak the language - even if it is just five minutes - and stick to it. This can mean for instance always speaking the language over breakfast, in the bath, or in the car.

Conversation can be encouraged through actual or even reverse bribery. You can make it clear that if your children make the effort to speak, they will be rewarded in an agreed way. Reverse bribery always makes me smile: children quickly learn that if they use the chosen language without prompting, our parental hearts will melt and they will be able to extract an impromptu reward. My friend Anna's boys have figured out that if, in passing a pick-and-mix display, they ask for a sweetie in French, smiling widely, they will automatically receive a positive response.

Any kind of conversation in a foreign language does have the tendency to drift back into English as soon as a lack of vocabulary becomes apparent, so it is useful to have a plan in advance as to how to deal with such a situation, e.g. refer to the dictionary or use the word in English and carry on in the foreign language. Be aware that speaking a foreign language will be tiring for both you and your child and it might be helpful to be flexible on timing if you or your child are too tired to make the effort.In one recent experiment, researchers found that "children could actively speak their second language if they were exposed to it for one-fifth of their waking hours[33]. If you cannot aim for this amount, be aware that your child might revert to their first language, and will require more active encouragement to speak back in the second language.

With the smallest babies, the melodic way parents tend to naturally speak with infants ("Motherese") is excellent for emphasising the cadence and rhythm of language which is such a fundamental part of the way people speak. As a baby grows and begins to speak, it is important (just as in your native language) not to try to correct sounds and words your children make in the new language, but to parrot and build the correct sounds and words into your responses. Similarly, if children mix up languages or make up words, the best response is to repeat the sentence correctly before going onto your response, in a way which

suggests that you are simply confirming what they have said rather than correcting them.

With the smallest babies, the melodic way parents tend to naturally speak with infants ("Motherese") is excellent for emphasising the cadence and rhythm of language which is such a fundamental part of the way people speak. As a baby grows and begins to speak, it is important (just as in your native language) not to try to correct sounds and words your children make in the new language, but to parrot and build the correct sounds and words into your responses. Similarly, if children mix up languages or make up words, the best response is to repeat the sentence correctly before going onto your response, in a way which suggests that you are simply confirming what they have said rather than correcting them. If you have time to plan such things, using a particular theme as a structure for learning is helpful. For instance, the boys were very excited to hear that we were going to go to the beach during the Easter holidays one year. On the way to the beach (a two-hour trip) they were happy to watch French DVDs with a beach theme in the car. On the beach we learned relevant words such as *la plage* (the beach), *le sable* (the sand), *le seau* (the bucket), and of course, *la glace* (ice cream). At home we could draw pictures of the beach and talk about what we did. All in all it was a great learning experience, a lot of fun, and a lot of French.

If you are bilingual, or nearly bilingual it might make sense to simply choose always to speak in the foreign language with your children. This is a kind of home language immersion programme. There are two versions of this - always to speak that language, but allow your children to speak to you in English - or to require them to speak back in the language. Either way, it is important to be consistent and firm, especially as children grow older and may choose to rebel against speaking another language, at least for a while. A nanny or relative with regular, close contact with your children might be able to provide a similar immersion experience.

As an example, when my father was 5 years old, he had a Spanish-speaking nanny for six months when his father had to travel away for business. Although my father has little recollection of the kind woman, he acquired an almost unconscious ability to speak Spanish nearly fluently, which he only discovered when he travelled to Spain years later.

Another way to provide your child with opportunities to converse, but outside the home, is to find a venue, such as a bilingual nursery or Saturday school, which provides an immersion experience. There, other people speak only your chosen language to your child.

The trickiest part of conversation is that it is one of the areas of language that requires frequent and regular practice. If you employ a Chinese nanny for one year and then they leave with no replacement, it is likely that no matter how fluent your child became during that period, they will start to lose that language facility rather quickly. Regular reinforcement is crucial.

Reading & writing

For the purposes of this guide, meant for children up to age 8, the emphasis on reading and writing is perhaps less than for older children. Nevertheless, there are many reasons why starting your children on this path is useful. One of these reasons is that books are an amazing, unrivaled source of vocabulary. However, learning to read is a tricky endeavour, even in your first language, so must be undertaken with some thought and care.

Lonsdale notes quite helpfully that "literacy follows fluency" i.e. it is easier to learn to speak before you learn to read rather than learn to read before you learn to speak.[34] This is therefore the first consideration: how far along your child is in learning to speak the second language. I would certainly suggest not trying to have your children learn to read in the second language before you reach the 100 word marker, or at least picking reading material in which the majority of the words are known.

The reason for this is that re-search has shown that reading - understanding and even just correctly guessing at the meaning of new words on a page - is difficult "unless one already knows 95 percent or more of the words in a text."[35] And, as we already know that a language learner has to come across a word up to 16 times before being able to regularly rec-ognise it, the only way it can work is to keep a dictionary and note-book at hand, a task which is more difficult for younger learners. It is perhaps therefore more ap-propriate to start reading and writing once your children enjoy a wider vocabulary of, say, 500 or more words

> ### Six Reasons for Teaching Reading in a Second Language
>
> *1. Reading is powerful - "the cornerstone of learning any language."*
> *2. Reading offers an additional and complementary kind of language exposure.*
> *3. Reading leads to increased vocabulary and better understanding, which in turn leads to greater facility and enjoyment when using the language.*
> *4. Reading leads to higher level language skills - "to make sense of complex language".*
> *5. Reading leads to increased cognitive benefits - "a challenging brain workout".*
> *6. Reading can help develop and safeguard language skills over a lifetime.*
>
> *- From Naomi Steiner's <u>Seven Steps to Raising a Bilingual Child</u>*

Once this intermediate hurdle is reached, the big debate becomes whether reading and writing should be introduced at the same time as your child is learning to read and write their first language, or afterwards. I per-sonally think that this decision has more to do with the per-sonality and learning style of each in-dividual child than to whether one or the other is objectively better. For my eldest I've chosen a more sequential approach (with the idea of introducing written French only after he has a strong basis in English phonics). My friend's child, Jessica, is very visual and enjoys learning through reading, so reading earlier works better for her. My Scott loves to write and is already scrawling down whatever words he knows, in whatever language, so it is easier to go with the flow than stop him in his tracks.

I think that in some ways the debate about when to introduce reading misses the point: that learning has to be fun, and fun and interesting games can be used to "teach" reading and writing in a language without the children really knowing that they are "learning". One April, when my eldest started to enjoy word searches in English I simply found a word search in French for him (on the theme of Easter), and he happily went about looking for *lapin* (bunny), *oeuf* (egg) and *panier* (basket). He didn't really notice that he was reading French for the first time. But I did!

As another example, the boys' French teacher, Nathalie, introduces the words for colours in colour - *bleu* in blue, *rouge* in red, *violet* in purple - so that children feel like they are reading when in part they are just saying what colour they see. This helps build their confidence in reading a second language at an early stage, which they just love.

Magnetic poetry (available to purchase online in many languages - and actually in many major supermarkets - or you can make your own) is a similar phenomenon. Why not every night put a simple sentence or poem on the fridge? When the children wake up in the morning, the magical appearance of new words (you might even suggest that fairies wrote it) will encourage them to try to read it. As you have complete control of the vocabulary, you can ensure you pick words that they already know.

Every so often, you could have a treasure hunt, with all the clues written in your chosen language. Or you could spend a few minutes a week labeling the items in one room of the house, and even leave the labels there for the week for the children to read over and over, at their leisure. Then, you can remove the labels and see if they remember, or make a little crossword puzzle for them to fill out at the end.

Again, here, our handy television comes into play with reading. As DVDs often come with language options for both the audio tracks and the subtitles, why not mix and match to encourage reading in both your mother tongue and the second language?

With regard to writing, again there are powerful reasons why it is beneficial to introduce it to children. It is important to remember, however, that particularly at the younger ages, it is primarily about communication, not about grammar and spelling.

Why not get the grandparents in on the game and have the children draw a picture, writing a little description or caption in the chosen language, to send to them? You could easily find a penpal in the country of choice, either through friends or through various reputable sites on the internet. A mythical figure would also do - if your child is young enough, you might want to suggest that Santa, the Tooth Fairy or the Easter Bunny (ignoring cultural traditions perhaps) speaks your chosen language and have the child write to them in that language.

For both reading and writing, character-filled activity books in the chosen language can be purchased, albeit it is easier to do so in the country (usually at the corner newsagent, as you would find in the UK), than on the internet. If you can, stock up when you are there or ask friends and family to purchase the appropriate aged magazines and colouring books if they are travelling to a country where that language is spoken.

These are just a handful of ideas that can make reading and writing fun, relevant and playful for your child, rather than a chore.

Some examples

Have I given you too many choices? Let me make it easier for you by giving you a few examples of what you might do, starting with my story.

When James was nearly three and Scotty nearly one, we started listening to "Baby's First Steps in French", a lovely CD with music and rhymes. We listened to it once or twice a week. In the meantime I set up a class in my home with a French native speaker for my children and four others, which met once a week term-time only. I also bought a few DVDs which I knew I could play in French. That was all I did for the first year. My children therefore both received about 4-5 hours of French a week during term-time, and a bit less over the holidays.

As my confidence has increased, and they have become a little older, we have added more to this mix. They are now completely used to watching DVDs in French, which is great - there is rarely any resistance when I put them on. We also play French children's music in the car for short journeys, although rarely around the house anymore. I have introduced a French games and songs website, on which Scotty plays maybe once a week. I also have some French books around the house, which we might read every so often. That increased their weekly input of French to maybe 6 hours. By giving them a choice of what to do, between reading in French, playing on a website or singing songs, the children are happier because they have been put in charge.

Just before Scott turned 4 years old and James 6, we went on a one-week holiday to France in which the children were in an all-French children's programme from 9 to 5pm. After that, I started speaking French to the boys in the car on the way to school - just 10 minutes a day. Then, over the summer, we were hanging out with a French friend who insisted on speaking French with the boys (and me!) exclusively, and we spent a long weekend in France. In the autumn, I asked the boys when else they might want to speak French, and they said on the way back from school in the car. So we have now added that into our daily (term-time) routine. Our weekly French input is perhaps now up to 7 or 8 hours, of which only 1 hour is a class.

Most recently, I enrolled the boys in a French Saturday school for bilingual children. They have fitted in fine and enjoy the chance to meet new friends. The Saturday school is focussed on helping them to speak, read and write, something that even bilingual families do not often find the time for. Importantly, I've managed to do this without sacrificing other important sporting activities, so that the boys do not miss out on other experiences.

In that time (just over four years) then, my boys have easily had about 1000 hours of French. My eldest, James, can now understand about 70% of what I say to him in French, and my youngest can understand about 30%. Both are happy to speak a few words or phrases a day, of their own volition, without any prodding from me. Scott has just started French in school, and is the star of the class - he loves it when the teacher asks him to show the class how to pronounce words properly!

As you can see, we just slowly and steadily built up our language activities over time - as and when it suited both myself and my children. I can honestly say that this has been done with little stress or strain on the boys or myself, and that there have been many extra benefits. For instance, James's school is planning a Spanish Club in the summer term of Year 2, and James is more or less chomping at the bit to start learning Spanish. He has none of the fear or reticence that we normally associate with language learning. Isn't that what learning should be all about? Fun, stress-free and fear-free. Free!

Susan's story

My friend Susan does not speak a second language, and has had very little chance to travel abroad. Nevertheless, she is extremely keen that her family, and her children in particular, travel abroad and learn about different cultures.

Susan set up a French class at home for her children when they were 1 and 3. With travel being a key component of her interest, Susan first arranged a day trip to Guernsey where they could try some French food and hear a little French being spoken. The family loved that, and following the children's interest in French, she booked a week outside Paris in a holiday cottage where the children could play with French children in the play park in the evenings. They helped the children order food and drink in French.

At home, Susan's children love the computer and often play on French game websites, and on French language CD-Roms. Her eldest likes to pretend to be a teacher and is often heard teaching her teddies colours and numbers in French. Susan says that "there are so many things I love about the kids' learning French. I love their confidence in speaking to French people when we are on holiday, and the encouragement they get in return. I love the fact that Jessica is so enthusiastic about languages that she is already looking forward to Spanish at school when it is offered next year. I love that Joe will count his cars in French. It has been a really good experience for us, and even been part of a wider family adventure to travel further afield."

Anna's story

Anna studied French at university and went on to purchase a holiday apartment in France. Her two boys have spent many holidays in France but she never actively tried to help them learn French. Then her eldest moved schools at the age of seven and actually struggled with the French lessons, partly because the children in his new class had been studying French for a year or so already. Anna realised that despite all the children's exposure to the language, they hadn't developed any confidence in language learning.

To head off this problem with her younger son, Anna decided to try three new tacks. First, she spent more time on holiday helping the children try out the language, for instance by helping them to order in French at restaurants and cafes. Her new rule was that they had to fend for themselves more.

Secondly, she set up a class at home with a French mum for the younger boy and his friends, in exchange for some babysitting. The children who attended the class played some football, spoke a little French and got rewarded with certificates and stickers when they learned something new. Inevitably the older boy picked up some of the vocabulary from the classes, but he was "too cool" to want to join in formally. With him, it was more a case of supporting the school work. This worked to the point that his confidence improved and his accent was complimented and he said "actually the teacher's accent is not as good as yours, Mum."

Thirdly, Anna set up a "French film" night, once a week at home. Her boys were encouraged to watch a fun film together with Anna one night a week. Asterix quickly became a favourite. She also introduced some fun language learning videos targeted at children, such as the Usborne 100 words in French DVD and playing familiar games in French.

Given that her boys were 7 and 3 when she started actively building French into their weekly schedule, Anna had to involve them very closely in the choices she made. She was very careful to work with the boys to find things that were enticing (football and films). As a result, ... Anna says "...it was trickier introducing activities when they were older because they were more resistant, but I really feel regular effort even at a fairly low level has paid off. It worked best when I focussed on what they thought was fun, rather than on what they had to learn."

Jonathan's story

Jonathan speaks French and Hebrew and lives in England with wife Yael and two boys. Jonathan and Yael speak Hebrew between them and initially did so with the boys. Eventually when the boys started school they stopped wanting to speak Hebrew, and even resisted being spoken to in Hebrew, saying they didn't understand. Jonathan wanted to speak more with them but didn't know there was an alternative to the "all or nothing" approach. Now he is committed to setting aside particular times of the day to speaking Hebrew with his children, and requesting material to be sent from Israel such as storybooks and DVDs. He hopes that this will help them restart their interest in Hebrew without putting any strain on their relationship.

Chapter 5: Summary

There are ten major tools and techniques that you can call upon to help your child learn a second language.

If you don't speak a second language yourself, or are just learning, don't just rely on once-a-week *classes: television, music, specialist language websites* and *holidays* all provide excellent entertainment for your children while they learn a second language alongside.

Books and *games* require a little more practice but nevertheless are easy to manage with a little preparation.

If you have enough confidence to speak the language yourself, even if you make mistakes, even a few minutes of *conversation* every day is a sure-fire method to engage your children as they will feel compelled to try to communicate with you, and in doing so will accelerate their learning.

The best approach is to try a little of everything, so that nothing becomes dull and you can see what works best for you and your child. If you have enough tools & techniques at your fingertips, you can mix and match to create an environment which provides both the repetition needed for learning, as well as the variation needed to keep everyone interested.

6. The language path: what to help them learn

As explained in Chapter 3, the path to learning a language starts with a child listening to a great deal of the language and then trying to copy the sounds. When learning a first language, babies babble away for hours trying to make the sounds. In a second language, with a more delayed start, toddlers might instead do what my Scotty did: speak English words with the new language accent. At one stage, if I pointed to a tomato and asked him *"c'est quel couleur?"* and the word *"rouge"* didn't come to him immediately, he might respond, "rrred" with a full-on French "r". He knew what it should sound like in French - he just didn't know the word.

This is a fantastic first step, which should be praised. But then it is your duty to help them find the words. Words are the primary building blocks for language: only once you know the words can you communicate.

Children start out with one word, two words, three words, and to them it is like an endless jigsaw puzzle. One piece, two pieces, three pieces - it is enough to see a little of what the puzzle is about, but not enough to put the puzzle together. The key is to reinforce the first few words - puzzle pieces - so they always have those at hand to use. Then add gradually, reinforcing all the time. Suddenly, parts of the puzzle start to come together, and you not only have *"chocolat"* but *"un chocolat chaud"* and finally, *"je voudrais un chocolat chaud"*.

You can see from this example that there are certain words that, in Lonsdale's terms, give you "leverage". [36] These are the words that allow your child to get the results he wants from communicating in the second language. The child that can make the sentence *"je voudrais un chocolat chaud"* is very likely to have a cup of hot chocolate delivered to him - a fabulous result if you happen to adore hot chocolate more than any other thing in the whole world.

The nice thing is that your child doesn't actually need too many words to get what he wants. Daily language generally is actually quite monotonous, limited to a small number of key items: some people, some objects, some actions, some descriptions, and a few extra "glue words" like "and" and "why", all of which help the jigsaw puzzle stick together[37]. It might be helpful for you to think through what your child might say on a daily basis (or what you might want to say to them) that would fall into these categories. Examples of the words Scott wanted to know included:

- **People:** I/me, you, he/she/they, Mum, Dad, brother, sister, teacher, friend, the Fat Controller, grandma
- **Objects:** This, that, chocolate, train, level crossing, chair, bowl, milk, music, car, toy, book, bath
- **Actions:** Go, stop, eat, drink, get up, sit down, play, can, want, draw, read, sleep, tickle, chase, peekaboo
- **Descriptions:** big/small, red/orange, hot/cold, on/off, yummy/yucky, too (as in too loud), still (as in hungry), sometimes, always, here/there
- **Connectors:** so, because, and, but
- **Questions:** who, what, when, where, why, how, how many, how old
- **Courtesy, greetings & praise:** Please, thank you, sorry, pardon, cheers, hello, how are you, good bye, well done, good job

If you build up your own list, you should come up with 100-200 words easily which you think you use every single day with your child. Think of these as your child's core vocabulary. They should be easy enough for you to learn and use regularly with your child. Once your child has achieved at a minimum some recognition of each of these words, you should find that they are both more enthused about the language and more focussed on listening, because they know they will be able to understand what you might be saying.

In order to help you along, I provide below some default lists that you can start with and modify according to your child's interests. The lists not only offer some suggestions for basic vocabulary but also some games you can play with your child to help them use them, repeatedly, in order to start to own them.

- **List 1 - First puzzle pieces:** This list is gives your child some simple words that they understand and can use all the time, thereby building confidence.

- **List 2 - Putting the puzzle pieces together:** This stage is about building vocabulary while giving your child some fun playing with simple sentences. By introducing short sentences early on, you can help them intuitively learn the different grammar structure of the new language.

- **List 3 - Expanding the size of the puzzle:** This stage is about building sentences into conversations by having fun with games, role playing and stories.

Games and activities are excellent for providing the necessary repetition to really own a word. I've suggested at least one activity or game for each type of vocabulary word that could be used to introduce it. It is not difficult to find songs for each topic as well, and it is just as easy to make them up. Use known tunes such as Old McDonald, Twinkle Twinkle Little Star, Baa Baa Black Sheep, B-I-N-G-O and anything else you can think of. I took both my boys to a baby sign language class when they were under 18 months, and the songs we used for that to learn the signs were almost all just pinched from the normal stock of nursery rhymes.

I should re-emphasise that these are just default lists, and really would be most effectively used if you modified them to suit your child. It would be no good teaching my Scott to say apples and oranges - he doesn't like them. However, he learned to say ham sandwich in an instant. James isn't much interested in trains, trucks and cars but will master the word for snowboarding in a flash.

The main emphasis is really on giving you some games and activities to use to help you build your child's vocabulary over time: from a word here and there to that magic 100 word target which will allow your child, with the right environment, to put the second language puzzle together by themselves.

List 1 - First puzzle pieces

In some ways, the first steps to language learning should be intuitive. What do baby books normally cover? Numbers, colours, animals, a bit of food, and family: mum, dad, granny, granddad. It is not surprising that these are often the first language topics covered in the national curriculum, so if you are keen that your child get ahead of what will be expected of him or her later on, these are the topics you will need to focus on.

Somewhat surprising is that some of the topics that are part of the normal day are not always covered early on in the language curriculum: sleeping, bathing and playing are three such examples. This is often because language learning still is primarily focussed on the older age groups, and somehow it is assumed not to be so necessary to be relevant and fun. I think this is a shame

One of the language lessons that my boys found most fun early on,

before they had mastered their numbers, before they had mastered their colours, was a little exercise of feeling particular objects to find out whether "*ça pique*" (it was sharp) or "*c'est doux*" (it is soft). To this day, after only 20 minutes playing with objects, they can still say "*ça pique*" and "*c'est doux*". Sensory involvement, music and physical effort all add so much fun to any learning that as far as I can tell they should be mandatory for at least part of any learning we do, whether we are young or old.

LIST 1: FIRST PUZZLE PIECES

Hello, My name is.../ Goodbye	Roll or throw a ball to your child. When they catch it, they have to say: hello, my name is. When they throw it to you, you have to say your name. Then allow them to use favourite character names, e.g. hello, my name is Bob the Builder.
How are you?	Draw pictures of a happy face, a sad face, an angry face, etc. Ask your child how they feel in the language, and ask them to point to the picture that represents how they feel.

Numbers 1-20	When tidying up: ask them to count how many cars/dolls/books they have lying about, and how many they have put away. Play hide & seek, where they have to count up to 10 before searching for you. Throw a die and ask them to tell you what the number is. Turn over playing cards one at a time - when your child can name the number correctly, he keeps the card.
Colours	Learn and then sing a rainbow song in your chosen language. Line up a number of coloured pens, get your child to close his eyes and then take one away, and see if they can guess which one is missing. Ask them if they are wearing anything red, and see if they can answer.
How old are you?	Draw a cake - let them pick how many candles they need, say how old they are, and then sing happy birthday with them and blow out the candles. Tease the child: say "you aren't 3, you are 5" and let them correct you.
Family members/ who is this?	Draw pictures of family members and ask them to guess who you've drawn.

Weather	Get a coat, an umbrella and sunglasses and put them about 10 feet away. When you say it's raining, have a race to get the umbrella and put it up. When you say it's sunny, race to put on the sunglasses.
First animals/ what is this?	Point to the animals and say "what is this?" Hide various animals around the house for a treasure hunt. Put a number of animals in a bag and the child can play with the ones that he picks out and names.
Please/thank you/excuse me/sorry	Give them a star or sticker each time they say please, thank you or excuse me in the right language (at the appropriate time).
Well done, good, great	Use these as much as possible!
Sensory words	taste (it's yummy/it's yucky), touch (hot/cold, rough/smooth), hearing (loud/soft), sight (big/little), smell (good/bad)Simply find things to taste, touch, hear, see and smell and get them to say what they think. If you participate as well, make sure to overemphasise your response and gestures (e.g. holding your nose if it smells).

Here are a few more games to play that might make it fun for all of you:

- One minute challenge: see how many words in a particular category they can name in one minute. Keep the scores and then play it again, showing them their progress. Another version of this is a word ladder race: draw a ladder and your child gets to move up a rung for each word they shout out.

- Play bingo with objects or animals: you call out the word, they have to recognise it and cover it on their card. A fun way to involve them in this from the start is to create the cards together.

- Drawing/colouring. You call out a word in the language and you both have to draw it (in the appropriate colour, if you called out a colour also). Another version of this is pictionary: you take turns drawing something and the other person has to call out what it is, in the chosen language.

- Making mistakes. A sure-fire winner that will leave you all in stitches is simply to make obvious and funny mistakes. Come in the door one day and say bye bye instead of hello. Point to a sheep and call it a cow. Point to grandma and call her grandpa! Count the people in the room and say there are ten rather than two. If you do it in an obvious way, they will giggle enormously - and correct you over and over again.

You can play these games as little or as much as you want: five minutes a week, or five minutes a day. As you know, small children have short attention spans but sponge-like brains, so if you keep it short and sweet you know they will take it all in.

Once they have mastered some of the vocabulary, you can build in a small conversation: hello, my name is..., I'm four years old. Another good step is to let them use the colours and numbers in conjunction with the animals or family members. Let them count one cow, two cows, three cows; or blue cow, red cow, white cow; or 3 blue cows, etc.

Once you have covered most of these subjects, even just once or twice, you should be ready to move onto the next stage.

List 2 - Putting the pieces together

This is where you move your child onwards from simple vocabulary building to speech. It is here where your child will learn - intuitively - the basic grammatical rules of the language, which can then become deeply embedded within their brains. So, just as you don't have to think to be able to conjugate "to be" (I am, you are, he is etc etc), or that the plural of sheep is well, sheep, they won't have to think to be able to do that in the second language - without having to learn by rote, which is how languages are taught later on in most secondary schools.

Language learning in schools and from books focusses very much on building vocabulary, often without the accompanying sentences. Your "Thousand Words in German" book is great as a dictionary, but less useful for real conversation. Encouraging your children to experiment with short sentences will give them an amazing headstart on language as they will be able to communicate their needs much more efficiently and effectively, and get better results from their efforts.

The aim of this next stage is therefore to start building simple sentences, using a wider range of vocabulary.

LIST 2: PUTTING THE PIECES TOGETHER

Clothes ("I put on my..., you take off your....")	Lay a bunch of clothes on the floor and play Simon Says, put on..., Simon Says, take off... Note what people are wearing when you are out and about. Dress up dolls & action figures.
Days/months/seasons ("Today is..., tomorrow will be..., yesterday was...")	Songs are great for learning these. Use a reward chart to make saying the day/date part of the daily activity. Use the weather words they learned to talk about the seasons, again making intentional mistakes. "In the summer it snows..." Make a poster for every season. Use major celebrations or events to talk about time: "what is tomorrow? Tomorrow is Daddy's birthday." Ask what they want to do in the morning, in the afternoon, in the evening - and if they get it right (and it is reasonable) they go do it!
Numbers 1-100	Take turns simply counting - children love to count over and over. Roll or throw a ball back and forth between you and count until you miss. Be mischievous and see if the children can guess how old people are. Count how many cars you see go by when you are off to the supermarket.

More animals (I see...)	Using props, play the memory game: I go to the zoo, and I see a lion. I go to the zoo, and I see a lion and a tiger. I go to the zoo, and I see a lion, a tiger and a hippo..." Actually go to a zoo or a farm and talk about the animals you see.
Parts of the body, & the phrases "I have an (ear ache)...", "I wash my (hands)"	Draw a monster with any number of eyes, ears, noses, arms, etc. Then ask them to describe it: my monster has one arm, two heads...." Play doctor, with bandages to wrap up parts of the body. In the bath, ask them to wash various parts of the body. Simon says, touch your toes.
Holidays/celebrations ("My favourite holiday is..., we eat... we do....")	Find out about the key features of the holiday in the country in question, and learn that vocabulary, with some props. Internet sites are great for providing activities and phrases that are appropriate for holidays, with plenty of free downloads.
Objects/rooms in the house ("I have a..., the chair is in/out, upstairs/downstairs, on top of, below...")	Draw a house together with any number of doors, windows, etc and say "my house has...". Hide a favourite toy around the house, and devise a treasure hunt. Start with "it is in the lounge" and then when they get there, add clues for where "under the pillow", "behind the sofa", on top of the shelf."

Food/drink: ("I like to eat/drink..., I like to buy, I like to cook...")	Play kitchen or shop. Bake something together. Set out some yummy food, and if they say the word in the right language, give them a bite to eat. Ask them what they like/don't like. Ask them what they think their doll/toy likes or doesn't like. You could even have a discussion as to what is healthy/not healthy. Play the memory "zoo" game with a food twist: "I went to the supermarket and I bought..."
Negatives: "I am/am not (hungry, thirsty, tall, old, tired)"	Each of you get a bag of objects, and then compare: "Do you have this? No, I don't have..." or "Do you like..., No, I don't like...." Look through a photo album of the family and state who is old, who is not, who is tall, who is not.
Games/toys: "I play (football), I play with my (bike, doll, train)".	Play toy tidy: go through your child's toys and state which ones he plays with and which ones he doesn't. Plan the summer holiday by talking about what games and sports you will play.
Places: "I go (to the shops, cinema, park, playground)."	With a cheap toy mat and a toy car, go exploring toy town. Pick just a few key places and ask them to say where they are going before they can move. Let your child help you plan jobs ("Shall we go to the supermarket now, or the post office?")

Singing nursery rhymes and reading simple picture books such as *Spot* is a great way to reinforce sentence building, as they are based on sentences rather than just word lists. If you do use vocabulary learning books, such as Usborne's 100 First Words series, try to use the vocabulary building to help your child build sentences. One easy way to do this is simply ask questions. For instance, if there is a page listing a number of different foods, point to foods you know your child does NOT like, and say "you like to eat...". They will immediately respond back, "no!" and if you are persistent, they will add "I don't like to eat ..., I like ..."

There is an excellent book in English called *You Choose* which Scotty loves, which is essentially a hundreds of pictures grouped into people, places, food, household objects, activities, jobs and more. With the express purpose of letting children build their own world with their own imagination, it has very few words so could be adapted for use in any language. Sit down with your little one, open the book and imagine together a new world... in your chosen language.

List 3 - Expanding the size of the puzzle

At this stage, the aim is to move gradually from simple sentences to building up conversations. This is most easily achieved through real activities, and where real activities are not possible, role-playing and story-telling.

A wider range of activities will start to introduce key concepts such as future and past tense, especially where there is a planning element. Once you have reached this stage, you know that you have succeeded in building your child's language foundation. They will have achieved a minimum set of vocabulary, begun to create real sentences, enjoyed playing in the language and taken a real interest in listening to and speaking in that language. You can pat yourself on the back - and then hopefully continue to slowly and surely build up their language proficiency.

LIST 3: BUILDING THE PUZZLE

Activities	Cooking together, nail painting, gardening, dressing up, building a train track In any activity, remind the child of the vocabulary first by making a list of everything that you need. Then find everything. If they want to participate in the activity (e.g. stirring the bowl, putting up a train track, etc.) they need to ask for it in the chosen language. Set a time limit (15 or 30 minutes), with a reward for participation at the end, e.g. first choice of cakes baked.
Holidays/celebrations	Hold a special holiday celebration from the chosen country, with as many of the its traditions as possible. Have a conversation about what is different and what is the same.
Trips out:	A picnic, a cafe or restaurant, a shopping trip, a beach trip: Take trips out but give them complete freedom to help you plan it (in the chosen language). Converse together about what to make or buy. Let them check what you already have and what you need to shop for. Make the trip out together, and then come back and talk about what you liked or didn't like about it.

Acting out stories:	Goldilocks etc: Pick out a few favourite classic stories and read them to your child. Build props together and then act out the story. Charades is a game you can play without props or cost, at any time, with a little practice on translating all the hand signals.
Playing board games:	Set out a games night, where you play in your chosen language. All the old classics are sure bets: Bingo, Lotto, Dominoes, Snakes & Ladders, Operation, Guess Who, etc etc. As your children get older, you could introduce (preferably by purchasing versions in your chosen language) Monopoly, Life, Risk, and Battleship, just to name a few.

In addition to the above, here are a few ideas I've cribbed from various places that you might like to build into your daily or weekly language activities:

- **Display Board**. Create, download or buy some colourful pictures for your focus area of the week or month, e.g. time/seasons. Put up the words you want to use as a reminder, as well as any activities you want to try.

- **Table mats**. Purchase, or print out and laminate, pictures of a few of your key focus areas (e.g. animals, food, even a map of the country) and put them out on the table at mealtimes to use as a fun attention grabber. Let them choose what mat to put out for each meal.

- **Word a day calendar**. Create your own calendar with the lists of vocabulary available on most websites. If your child can name the word(s) at the end of the day, give them a penny for their piggy bank.
- **Car games**: "I spy" and "who am I" are classic car games that can be used even from stage 1, focussing on the vocabulary they already know. Mix English and the language if you find it easier, for instance asking questions in English (is the person a boy or a girl?) to reach the answer in the chosen language (grandpa - grandpere).
- **Object poke no backs**: if you see a particular object and can say it (in the chosen language) before the other person, you can poke them without retribution. Kids love to have the license to bully you! This is great for walks in the park, for instance, first to see a squirrel, a dog, the ice cream van, etc.
- **Night time song/lullaby**. Sing a lullaby in the chosen language at bedtime. It is a perfect time because all your children want is to hear your voice, singing softly to them: they are the only people in the world that don't mind if you are out of tune. Make the most of it, and put it into your routine.

As you can see, most of this list is just games you would play with your child anyway: the only difference is that it is in a different language. You are not missing out on any other activities, "hothousing" them into learning vocabulary lists, or stigmatising them socially as the sceptics might suggest. You are simply having fun!

Chapter 6: Summary

Ideally, the path to learning a language should be led by your child: what interests them, and what topics excite them at the moment: trains and cars, dolls and babies, sharks and dinosaurs. These should be considered to be pieces of their little world, which you can help them discover and use in the chosen language. As they learn more and more words for these pieces, they can start putting the pieces together, and finally building the full language picture themselves.

Initial pieces might include numbers, colours, family members and greetings. Putting these pieces together with other ones is the next step: one dog, red strawberry, funny music, sore toe. Finally, build these pieces into real communication: full sentences such as "I want that present" and "when is Santa coming" won't be far off if you choose your subjects carefully.

Activities and games are an excellent way to engage your child because they are fun yet often repetitive, allowing plenty of practice to embed the words into your child's brain. You know you are on the right track when you make mistakes (either on purpose or accidentally) and they correct you, giggling all the way.

7. Potential problems with & how to overcome them

In a perfect language-learning world, we would be fluent in the language we are trying to teach our children; we would have the full backing of the (also fluent) local community, schools and extended family; we would have all the resources we needed at our fingertips; and our darling children would love the new language and take every opportunity to speak, read and write it.

Sigh. Okay, the world isn't like this. But, hey, if you are reading this you probably already know that and, as an added bonus, you probably like the challenge. Here are some of the obstacles you might have to overcome:

- Lack of fluency
- Lack of support
- Lack of motivation
- Lack of co-operation
- Lack of progress
- Stuttering and hearing problems

Lack of fluency

Unfortunately, we live in a highly self-conscious society. We worry what others think of the way we walk, the way we dress, and of course the way we talk. This last issue becomes severely heightened when we are trying to speak another language. First, we have our internal demons insisting that our accent is poor, our vocabulary is too limited, our grammar is atrocious, so how can we even think we could pass this on to our children.

So, without stepping outside our doors, we already have hurdles to overcome. Luckily, my children absolutely love it when they pick up on my mistakes and poor accent, as they revel in correcting me. So not only do I have to put up with my children telling me that I really must learn English properly and not speak American all the time, they are now telling me that my French accent is poor and I must practice more. Heave sigh....

Once we extend language learning outside the home, the issue becomes much more real: other people can hear us then! What will so-and-so think if I speak such poor French with my child, I would shudder, as I dropped the kids off at school. Will they hear how poor my French is and think I am silly for trying to speak French? Will they think I am trying to show off? Will they think I am one of those "hothouse" parents who can't just let their children grow up "normally"?

With regard to speaking outside the home, I admit that even I, generally the type to ignore public opinion in matters of fashion and decorum, still feel a tad silly speaking to my children in French at the school gates. Nonetheless, to my surprise, most of the reactions I get are very positive. People either think that I have a French background (very flattering indeed) which I am stalwartly trying to pass on to my children, or they don't notice. Seriously, most people don't even pay attention if you are speaking another language. And if they do notice, most don't even care.

So the moral of this story is, drop the self-consciousness. Your children won't be harmed by your mistakes, and to be frank, no one else cares. It would be a shame to lose such a marvelous opportunity to improve your children's lives, just because you were too shy.

Lack of support

This year I decided to move my language goals up one notch and to speak French in the car to my children simply during the morning run to school. The children seemed to accept this, albeit sometimes grudgingly. I managed to piece together a few set phrases (always noting the weather, the traffic, and the fact that we were almost there!). They spoke back to me mostly in English. Soon, however, my fleeting attempts were getting a bit more fluent, and with every encouraging noise from me a few French words seemed to be creeping into our conversation from their side which made me quite pleased with the progress. Even Scotty, my four year old, who was initially quite grumpy about the whole plan, started actually getting excited about it. Wow!

Then one day my husband Trev chose to come to school with us. He was looking forward to being part of the school run, and for a few more minutes with his beloved boys. He wasn't even aware that I had been speaking French to them in the car, and then when I told him just before getting in the car, he quickly agreed to try to speak French too. However, three minutes into the journey, and after struggling himself for a minute, he burst out that he couldn't believe that speaking in French in the car meant a 15 minute French monologue from me and well he wasn't going to do it. He wanted to be able to speak with his boys as well, and couldn't do it in French. For the rest of the journey he spoke in English with the kids and I just fumed in my seat. For the next week, my husband's outburst still lingered, and the children refused to engage in French games in the car.

Well, as you can imagine, that is something that could have made me give up this new effort. I could have blamed my husband, but in fact it was *my* fault. I had not fully explained what I was doing to Trev and why I was doing it; I had not made him aware of the benefits; I had not prepared him for the car journey, especially when he was so looking forward to the extra few minutes with his boys. He had felt left out and indeed was baffled as to how this would help the boys learn French.

From this, I learned an important lesson: even the most well-meaning people (and Trev really is well-meaning) need guidance if they are to provide any support for your goals and aspirations. Support from close family and friends is an important aspect of language learning, as their enthusiasm and support will help bolster the children's own feelings about language learning, even if they do not speak the language themselves.

If you choose to involve family and friends, do take the time to explain to them why on earth you are trying to teach them a new language. Ask permission to speak the language with your child in front of them, and translate where necessary so they don't feel left out. Let them know what you think the benefits will be. If necessary, ask them to show enthusiasm for the process as well, so the children can see that the language experience will get them positive feedback from others as well as yourself. Try to give them some guidance as to how to deal with the children when they are trying to speak another language, for instance if (as happens often) the children mix up words between their mother tongue and the new language, or if they make a grammatical mistake or error in pronunciation. The more information your support network has, the more supportive they will be.

You need to decide to whom you need to give this explanation and guidance. I told all the people who came into regular, close contact with my boys, including primary teachers and caregivers. This meant that when my eldest came into school singing a French nursery rhyme, or counted in French, he could be praised for it rather than (at best) be met with a blank stare.

Of course, there are some people whom you will never convince: the ones that say that learning a second language confuses children, or that English is going to rule the world anyway so why bother. If you cannot minimise contact with such people, for instance the difficult mother-in-law who comes over for Sunday lunch, and you still want to minimise the conflict that it might cause either between you or between those people and your children, then it might be necessary, as a last resort, to (slightly) alter your learning plans to avoid such conflict.

I have found that for the most part people are incredibly supportive and accommodating - for instance quite happy to have you speak to your children in a different language without feeling left out - if they understand your goals and how you are planning to achieve them.

Lack of motivation

Let's not kid ourselves: it is very easy to lose motivation in this area. There are an untold number of competing priorities that we need to contend with as parents. As a person very committed to language learning, I am also naturally enthusiastic about learning in general. I love it when my children show interest in music, maths, sports or any number of specific subjects such as sharks, or outer space. As a person who just needs to relax, like anyone else, sometimes the added pressure of trying to find just the right way to introduce French into our daily lives can be a strain.

The easiest way to keep up motivation is to get into a routine. If your language learning is set for always a particular place, or a particular time, then it becomes easier for you and more acceptable for the children. Never-theless, it is still easy to fall off the language train. When my children first received a DVD as a present - in English - I didn't want to take it away from them. They played it until they were tired of it - then I put the French DVDs back on. When my children started to ask for pop music in the car - in English - I didn't want to take the pleasure away (theirs and mine) of hearing them sing "oo oo baby, slap my thigh" at the top of their lungs. Again, as they tired of it, I reverted to French. When my son wanted to hear "times tables" songs during our usual French song time, which then was more important - his enthusiasm for

maths, or my enthusiasm for French? In this case, maths took precedence (at least, until I could find another time of day to play it).

Also, if you have had a bad night's sleep, speaking a second language in the car might be the last thing you have energy for. If you have had a hard day's work, just keeping the kids quiet in front of the television (in English) might be just what you need. In these cases, give yourself a break, with the *explicit* - i.e. spoken - understanding that it will be back to normal when you are back to normal.

The message here is to be gentle with yourself. Accept that at times you will not be able to live up to the high standards you expect of yourself as a parent, and then, when you do have the energy, start again.

I am constantly amazed by how accepting my children are of my lapses in routine. When I am ready again, they fit right back into it again, with hardly a whimper. The key, again and again, is to find your own internal enthusiasm and positive energy that the children can soak up while they are learning.

> *Once acquired, an extra language is like swimming or dancing or bicycling, in not being easily forgotten in disuse. But for successful and skillful performance, it requires, like these, constant practice and effort.* [40]

Lack of co-operation

Trev, my husband, has a favourite home mantra: "This is NOT a democracy." With this young age group, rules and boundaries are set all for almost everything. You will NOT bounce on the sofa. You will say please and thank you. You will come to the dinner table when called. We all know that children do not obey orders like soldiers, and that there is some give and take. But for the most part, it is important to treat the rules and boundaries you set for language learning just like any other rule you set. If children turn the television on in English, and the rule is television in French, then you must treat the action as you would treat any rule break, e.g. turn off the telly, a time out, etc.

If one of the rules is that the children themselves must speak your chosen language, then from time to time they will try English. If they are just asking you for a word, that is fine. If they are refusing to speak the language required, then you have to decide as a parent whether this is something that is simply a small act of rebellion, or whether something more serious (e.g. teasing at school, or an undermining relative) might be behind it. For the rebellious act, it is enough at times just to name it as such, explain your expectations and carry on.

For the more serious issues, it is important as in any other area of parenting to be sensitive to the problems: once a problem is unearthed, it can be resolved, and your day to day routines can then be re-established. For instance, some parents, who speak to their children in one language at home while their children converse in another language at school, might at one point or another find that their child refuses to speak the home language. This could be a simple act of rebellion, but it could point to issues the child is having at school: perhaps they are finding classwork difficult in the new language, or lack of teacher training in how to help your child when language issues arise. The best way to deal with this is to speak to your child's teacher, define the problem, and look for a solution. The solution certainly does NOT have to be to completely stop speaking the home language at home, although teachers without knowledge of second languages may recommend that. It may mean extra help for a temporary period for your child while they adjust. As school time is an important part of your child's emotional, social and academic development, it is an issue that should be addressed as soon as possible.

Often I find that children just like to have options. Recently, my boys wanted a break from speaking French in the car. I said, fine, if they agreed to read a book in French every night instead. They were happy because I listened to their request and honoured it; I was happy because we were doing something different and just as valuable.

One of the less serious but tricky problems to deal with is if your child simply gets bored with whatever routine you've set up. If you have set up Friday night as French DVD night, and all of a sudden they get tired of the telly, and want to spend Friday evenings on the Wii or on the computer. You then lose a cornerstone of your language learning routine.

Children do have a tiresome habit of growing up and wanting to do new things. This is where accessing a wide range of language sources is important. It is not that they are necessarily tired of the language - they are tired of the medium, or the material. Get something new - subscribe to a language website, find some audiobooks, take out some simple board games - and they will be newly inspired. Not necessarily by the language in and of itself, but by the fun that the language game can be - and the parent-child sharing time that goes with it. If you make it fun, they will do it. As simple as that.

One of my friends uses a penalty system for swearing: if you are heard swearing, you have to put a penny in the jar, and that jar is then used to buy treats for the whole family. Why not use it for language learning? If it is the designated time to speak a language, and one of you doesn't, then you have to put a penny in the jar. Children love to catch you out: if you make mistakes and have to add to the jar they will love the game and want to play. Another system for smaller children might be just to designate a policeman to catch the language rule breakers for the day. Any tool like this is great for motivating the more competitive children especially.

Lack of progress

Language learning is not unlike other areas of skill acquisition for children - sometimes you might go for months and months without any noticeable difference or improvement. With infants and babies, pre-speech, the wait for any sign of understanding or verbal response can seem eternal. And children are very different: my eldest, James, loved to use his new French vocabulary immediately; my youngest felt left out for awhile, and purposely excluded himself from French conversations out of a combination of rebelliousness, shyness and lack of knowledge. No one, however, likes to be on the bench forever, and eventually everyone comes out to play the game - especially when it is all play and no work! Scott may have felt left behind, and only really started to come out of his shell when he started French at school - when I believe he finally felt like a star player rather than the last one out of the block.

> *The path through language acquisition is not necessarily smooth and even. Learners have bursts of progress, then seem to reach a plateau for a while before something stimulates further progress.*[41]

Patience and persistence is therefore crucial, but a supportive environment is also important. James's teachers confided in me that when French lessons started in Reception the other children who spoke different languages felt more comfortable expressing their own cultures and vocabulary. Suddenly, the classroom became enthused about languages and cultures and every child came out of him or herself a bit more - creating an environment in which all children could progress.

Patience and persistence is therefore crucial, but a supportive environment is also important. James's teachers confided in me that when French lessons started in Reception the other children who spoke different languages felt more comfortable expressing their own cultures and vocabulary. Suddenly, the classroom became enthused about languages and cultures and every child came out of him or herself a bit more - creating an environment in which all children could progress.

It is important to recognise as well that your child may be learning a tremendous amount subconsciously through comprehension practice - in other words, just through listening. He may not demonstrate it through speech, but his head he may be racking up the times he has come across key words, until he hits some magic number and the words suddenly become consciously accessible. The name of the game is to never underestimate how much a child learns through listening.

Stuttering & hearing problems

There is some debate as to whether using a second language in the home can induce a period of stuttering in the child at a certain age (3-5 years old), in both languages. This is potentially caused by something called cognitive overload [38], a temporary issue at age 3-4. Both my children stuttered slightly in English at that age (in endearingly different ways) and it was clear from listening to them that it was caused by the struggle to find the vocabulary conflicting with their desire to express themselves. I can easily see how this would be magnified by having a larger jumble of vocabulary in which to lose themselves. In extreme cases, it may be necessary to halt the use of a second language for a short period of time until the stuttering ceases. Two separate friends, who were both trilingual, chose to *temporarily* suspend the use of the third language with their children at this age for this reason. Nevertheless, this is not an issue for the vast majority of people using more than one language at home.

Hearing problems, as you can imagine, are a different issue. Young children can suffer from temporary hearing loss, as the shape of the young ear canal is more susceptible to ear infections, glue ear and the like. The problem with any hearing loss at this age is that, apart from the general learning and social effects, the window to learn to hear sounds properly is limited, so the sooner such problems are diagnosed, the better the child will learn to hear and speak any language later in life.

For children learning multiple languages, there is a risk that hearing problems can be overlooked as language mix-ups and mispronunciations are more common. Teachers, who are often the first to pick up hearing issues (parents have less comparison points) may assume that the language problems they see are due to the second language learning rather than to any hearing loss. If you have any concerns, however small, have your child's hearing checked by a specialist through a referral from your GP.

You can come out now Johnny. Senorita Pena left three hours ago.

7: Summary

Helping a child learn a language is not always a cake walk. First you have to deal with your own issues:

- Lack of fluency
- Lack of support
- Lack of motivation

Then you have to deal with your child's issues:

- Lack of co-operation
- Lack of progress
- Stuttering and hearing problems

Some of these problems can be serious, and require direct intervention. The serious ones, however, have less to do with language itself and more to do with you and your child's happiness, health and environment. If you can keep yourself and your child healthy, happy and well-supported, then both of you can have fun learning a language.

A good lesson for anything else you choose to do.

8. An appealing conclusion

If there is one clear message I hope you have understood from this book, it is that I think that language learning is fun, exciting, worthwhile and easily achievable for your child, no matter your own background in languages.

Teaching your children a second language is not difficult, but it takes time. Just like teaching them to swim, or bicycle, or read. A language, like these skills, requires practice and effort, and like these skills, becomes more and more enjoyable the more accomplished your child becomes.[39] If you make this practice and effort just another part of their daily life, like getting dressed, or having a bath, they will accept it as part of their life and it won't feel like a chore. Keeping it fun, lighthearted and interesting might be the hard part for you, but it is worth the effort on your part to make it effortless for them.

There is so much to gain, and it is in the little wonders that we can revel. As our children progress from understanding a few words, to speaking, to conversing, and even reading or writing a little, we the parents can continue to emphasise the enthusiasm that we feel about learning languages. If we can make it fun, and they can gain confidence, as they approach eight years old they will have a marvelous foundation: they will have learned that languages are exciting and that they are *good* at languages, before language education in school kicks in and (in some cases) does its damage by making it formal, dry and uninspired. Your efforts in their early years should help give them the motivation to continue learning languages throughout life.

Remember, full fluency is not necessary for our communication with anyone: how often is it that a simple conversation about the weather is enough to enjoy being with a friend or acquaintance. A few words and phrases allow us to break the ice and begin to relate to our fellow human beings.[42] Providing children with the opportunity to move from our

English comfort zone into a new environment, to relate to others, to create new links, to achieve, to become self-confident: all these goals become attainable with the introduction, little by little, step by step, of another language.

This is the goal to which we all - not just lucky bilinguals - can aspire, and most importantly, just like learning to bicycle - we can enjoy together with our precious children.

An appeal for a radical rethink

I have been writing this book as a debate rages in the UK educational establishment: should younger children be in school at all? If in Germany children don't start formal education until they are 7, why are British children, who start as young as 4, not way ahead? What benefit - or indeed disbenefit - are our children getting from their early start in formal education?

Now, as you have already probably guessed, I am a big proponent of early education. I think that children are sponges and are not only ready but have an incredible hunger to learn, right from the time they can focus their eyes and distinguish different sounds. We need to take advantage of this learning, and there is no reason why this learning cannot take place in a school environment.

The key question for me is not whether they should be learning but indeed what. Reading, writing and arithmetic? Or a second language?

I cannot shake off Pinker's weighty conclusion in his book, where he remarks that the "three-year-old... is a grammatical genius ... [however is] notably incompetent at most other activities."[43] It is indeed amazing that a three-year old, who can barely count to 10, let alone read or write, can speak his native tongue fluently. It seems daft, doesn't it, to let this natural talent go to waste, when other languages are so easily picked up.

Our nurseries and pre-schools obviously haven't read Pinker. Literacy and numeracy begin to take centre-stage before children even have their nappies off.

From a literacy point of view, there is a very strong emphasis on learning to read and write English from pre-school onwards. Unfortunately, it is not at all proven that children actually benefit from an early start in these areas. Indeed, children who start later often catch up with the early birds within half a year to a year.

There are many possible reasons for this, but I'll mention just two: one which affects reading, and one which affects writing. As I mentioned in Chapter 5, literacy follows fluency: it is easiest to learn how to read *after* you learn how to speak. More specifically, even preschool reading books use a lot of words that children have not yet come across in their speaking lives. Give those children a few more years, and they will read those words more easily simply because they can recognise them.

Regarding writing, I personally am concerned with the issue of fine motor skills development. This is the development of the muscles that control small movements, such as pencil strokes. My oldest boy James is somewhat delayed in his fine motor skill development, which means that his writing is not as neat as his classmates. Although his teachers are very encouraging, he nevertheless struggles to keep up in class when having to write notes down from the board or do spelling tests. I have to remind myself that were he in Germany he wouldn't be in school at all at the moment, and the pressure on him would be much lighter. Instead of struggling, he might be spending more time colouring and other activities that would help him develop his fine motor skills without the pressure to produce something specific and legible in a short amount of time.

On the numeracy front, again there is a significant pressure during the early education years on recognising numbers, counting up to a certain point, addition and subtraction. Yet again sometimes there is a question as to whether starting early on the theory of numbers detracts from the practical knowledge children need to gain at an early stage: being able to understand real mathematical problems and solve them (Scotty's favourite: the sweet machine requires 20p, how many seconds does it take for him to find coins that add up to 20p in mum's purse), or osmosing the understanding of mathematics through a much more accessible but very mathematical medium: music.

And yet, the one thing that young children are already plenty ready to do - learning a second language - is relegated to Key Stage 2!

And unfortunately, many children learn to hate it, partly because as they get older and older, it is harder and harder to learn a second language. As Pinker rightly emphasises, "....it is much more difficult to learn a second language in adulthood.... Most adults never master a foreign language, especially the [sounds] - hence the ubiquitous foreign accent.... [T]here seems to be a cap even for the best adults in the best circumstances."

This is the trap that we are setting for our children, if we don't make the effort to give each and every child a chance to learn a language early. Pinker goes on to suggest a key factor in why children are so gifted in languages: "sheer age."[44]

In fact, Pinker cites studies[45] showing that "the acquisition of normal language is guaranteed for children up to the age of six, is steadily compromised from then until shortly after puberty, and is rare thereafter...." Other studies have also shown that age limits definitely apply to the mastery of any language, especially its grammar, pronunciation and intonation.[46]

Pinker suggests that *learning* a language is in effect a "one-shot skill." We learn grammar quickly, and the only thing that we continue to build on over time is vocabulary. The parts of the brain that are used to acquire language therefore become redundant, and for reasons of survival-of-the-fittest "should be dismantled if keeping it around incurs any costs."[47]

In other words, right now our education system actually begins to teach our children a second language *at the very point* their brains start forgetting how to do it. And our education system begins to teach our children literacy and numeracy *at the very point* children find it most difficult.

It is not that older children (say, 10-15 years old) don't stand a chance when in comes to learning a language. Indeed, many of them are used to structured learning and therefore, *if they are motivated*, can pick up the basics of a language even quicker than younger children. What they cannot then go on to do is fully master the language[48]. And what you cannot do, as a parent of a child at that age, is help them as much with their motivation.

It strikes me that we are actually causing some children damage through too much focus on numeracy and literacy in the early years, while not taking advantage of an easy early win that will serve children well throughout their lives.

My humble opinion is that we should radically rethink not when we put our children in school but what we expect them to learn. Let us make learning a second language not just a part of, but a *cornerstone* of Early Years and Key Stage 1 education. It makes perfect sense to me for children to learn something that their whole bodies are yearning to pick up at these early stages, and give their minds and bodies time to grow into literacy and numeracy before expecting too much from them.

What do I mean by "a cornerstone?" Research shows that our current "drip-feed", one-hour-per-week approach to learning languages - no matter how young children start - will not produce advanced language learners. On the other hand, a period of intense learning, even if followed by a lighter schedule, often has a significantly better effect on mastery of the language[49]. Why not provide our youngest children - in our nurseries, pre-schools and through Key Stage 1 - a minimum of one to two hours *per day* of language learning. This will not interfere with those politically-motivated goals of literacy and numeracy, and can be built into other important but sadly neglected areas such as art, music and outdoor play.

The stakes these days cannot be higher. Our world is increasingly global and yet we are raising children who are not prepared for it, and indeed, unfortunately, fear it - fear speaking a new language, fear thinking in a new way, fear foreigners themselves.

If you pick up this book, and enjoy using it to help your child learn a language, why not speak to your child's nursery and school at the outset about what they can do to introduce a second language at the earliest possible point. And if you are politically minded, write to your MP. It might be something, eventually, we can get right for our children. In the meantime, your child's language education is in your hands. Make the most of it!

9. References & Resources

Today the resources required to support language learning are completely at our fingertips. The following list is just the tip of the iceberg of what is available. For more detailed information on, and links to, language learning resources, please see www.languages4yourkids.com.

Books:

Baker, Colin. *A Parents' and Teachers' Guide to Bilingualism*. Multilingual Matter Ltd. 1995.

Harding, Edith and Riley, Philip. *The Bilingual Family: A Handbook for Parents*. Cambridge University Press, 1995.

Haugen, E. 1953, *The Norwegian Language in America: A Study of Bilingual Behavior*. 2nd Printing, Revised 1969. Bloomington: Indiana University Press.

King, Kendall and Alison Macey. *The Bilingual Edge: Why, When, and How to Teach Your Child a Second Language*. HarperCollins, 2007.

Lightbown, Patsy and Nina Spada. *How Languages are Learned*. Third Edition. Oxford University Press, 2006.

Lonsdale, Chris. *The Third Ear*. Third Ear Books, 2006.

Pinker, Steven. *The Language Instinct*. Penguin Books, 1994.

Saunders, George. *Bilingual Children: Guidance for the Family*. Multilingual Matters Ltd.

Steiner, Naomi, MD, with Susan L Hayes. *7 Steps to Raising a Bilingual Child*. Amacom, 2008.

Tynan, Bernadette. *Make Your Child Brilliant*. Quadrille Publishing Limited, 2008.

Useful general language websites:

For games and more, try:

- BBC Languages http://www.bbc.co.uk/languages/ for adults and http://www.bbc.co.uk/schools/websites/4_11/site/languages.shtm for children.
- Hello World http://www.hello-world.com (subscription only).
- LCF Clubs: http://www.lcfclubs.com (subscription only).
- Digital Dialects http://www.digitaldialects.com/index.htm - This has some good audio games, and though they are not specifically directed to children they are easy to understand and do.
- Word2Word http://www.word2word.com/ . This site has links to many other sites, including youtube videos, games and more.

For translations and vocabulary, try:

- Babel Fish Translation http://babelfish.altavista.com/

- Jennifer's Language Page
  http://www.elite.net/~runner/jennifers/ . This site is good for
  basic greetings & vocabulary in hundreds of languages.
- Language Guide http://www.languageguide.org. This site has
  some excellent audio files for help with pronunciation of basic
  words, and readings, but no pictures.
- Reall Languages http://www.reall-languages.com/languages.htm
  . This site has audio files for basic words, for help with
  pronunciation, and games (although the games have no audio, so
  reading skills are required).

Primary school materials:

- Primary school language support:
  http://www.newburypark.redbridge.sch.uk/langofmonth/
- Dual Language Posters
  http://www.schoolslinks.co.uk/resources_dl.htm. This has
  posters as well as further language site links.

Online specialist shops and language support for parents and teachers:

- Foreign Language Fun: http://foreignlanguagefun.com
- Languages For Your Kids: http://www.languages4yourkids.com
- Linguatots: http://www.linguatots.co.uk
- Little Linguist: www.little-linguist.co.uk

Useful specific language websites:
One Website For Each Language (From:
http://www.newburypark.redbridge.sch.uk/langofmonth/activitiesbook
let.pdf)

- Afrikaans http://www.easyafrikaans.com/easyafrikaans/index.html
- Arabic http://muttaqun.com/arabic/
- Bengali http://www.virtualbangladesh.com/bd_bhasha.html
- BSL http://www.britishsignlanguage.com/words/index.php?id=337
- Cantonese http://www.chinese-lessons.com/index.htm
- Czech http://www.bfinclusion.org.uk/EAL%20files/Resnewtoeng.htm
- Dutch http://learndutch.elanguageschool.net/
- Finnish http://www.uuno.tpu.fi/
- French http://www.bbc.co.uk/schools/primaryfrench/
- German http://www.bbc.co.uk/languages/german/index.shtml
- Greek http://www.bbc.co.uk/languages/greek/
- Gujarati http://gujaratonline.com/index.html
- Hebrew http://www.learn-hebrew.co.il/
- Hindi http://www.hindilearner.com/
- Indian Languages, http://www.languageshome.com.
- Italian http://www.bbc.co.uk/languages/italian/index.shtml
- Japanese http://japanese.about.com/
- Lithuanian http://www.slic.org.au/Language/
- Mandarin http://www.bbc.co.uk/languages/chinese/real_chinese/
- Nepali http://learnnepali.com/index.html
- Norwegian http://www.sofn.com/norwegian_culture/languagelessons_index.jsp

- Polish http://info-poland.buffalo.edu/web/travel/polish/link.shtml
- Portuguese http://travlang.com/languages/
- Punjabi http://www.punjabonline.com/servlet/index
- Romanian http://www.linguata.com/romanian/Learning_Romanian.html
- Russian http://masterrussian.com/
- Sinhala http://www.speaksinhala.com/
- Slovak http://www.bohemica.com/slovak/
- Spanish http://www.bbc.co.uk/languages/spanish/
- Swahili http://www.glcom.com/hassan/swahili.html
- Tamil http://ccat.sas.upenn.edu/plc/tamilweb/
- Thai http://www.learningthai.com/speak_thai.html
- Turkish http://www.onlineturkish.com/
- Urdu http://www.urduword.com/

Acknowledgements

This book could not have been written without the unfailing support of my husband, Trev, who provided constant encouragement, and my mother, Adi, who not only helped with editing but also printed advance copies to give out to her friends and thus prodded me to publish. Joleene Naylor provided invaluable help in formatting and Paul Wilcox turned my rough ideas into sparkling cartoons. Last but not least, my sons James and Scott deserve special thanks for being my guinea pigs.

...Catching Tongues by Carolyn Gibson ...

Endnotes:

1 - I fail to mention here that Nadine and Iain, my fabulous stepchildren, came to live with us when they were aged 7 and 11. I also helped them learn French, however due to their ages when we began, their story is for another book. Sorry guys!

2 - The word "bilingual" has many different definitions but it is most commonly used, in my experience, to describe people who are native or near-native speakers of two languages. I have never considered myself to be bilingual, as despite my long endeavours, my second language, French, still requires much effort and is full of mistakes.

3 - Colin Baker, p. 40.

4 - Colin Baker, p. 47-8.

5 - George Saunders.

6 - Lightbown, p. 62.

7 - Lonsdale, p. 41.

8 - Lonsdale, p. 38-9.

9 -Lonsdale, p. 34.

10 - Lightbown, p. 40.

11 - Speaking of standing on the shoulders of giants, it is worth noting that Pinker uses as his starting point Chomsky's Universal Grammar concept.

12 - Lightbown, p.3.

13 - Lightbown p. 98.

14 - Lonsdale p. 78.

15 - Lightbown p.188. "Research on pronunciation has shown that second language speakers' ability to make themselves understood depends more on their ability to reproduce the phrasing and stress patterns - the 'melody' of the language - than on their ability to articulate each individual sound."

16 - For an average toddler, "about half the words are for objects: food, body parts, clothing, vehicles, toys, household items, animals, and people. ...There are words for actions, motions, and routines, like up, off, open, peekaboo, eat and go, and modifiers, like hot, all gone, more, dirty and cold. Finally, there are routines used in social interaction, like yes, no, want, bye-bye, and hi." Pinker p. 266-7.

17 - Pinker, p. 237.

18 - Pinker p. 281.

19 - Lightbown, p. 11-14.

20 - Lonsdale, p. 158.

21 - Pinker, p. 150.

22 - Lightbown, p. 96-7.

23 - Pinker, p. 32

24 - Lonsdale p. 47.

25 - Lightbown p. 145-150.

26 - Lightbown p. 152.

27 - The exception I made to this rule is sign language: I did baby signing with both my boys from 6 to 24 months. I felt that (a) it helped us communicate better before they could speak, (b) it could be done alongside French, and (c) it was another way for them to learn that the same concept can be conveyed in different ways - the precursor to speaking another language.

28 - King, p. 115.

29 - Steiner p. 27.

30 - Tynan, p. 12.

31 - From: Monique Barb, "Children and Their Particularities of Age in Teaching a Foreign Language" from: http://articles.famouswhy.com/

32 - King p. 104.

33 - King, p. 107.

34 - Lonsdale, 54.

35 - Lightbown, p. 100.

36 - Lonsdale, 91.

37 - Lonsdale, 133.

38 - Baker, p. 101.

39 - Haugen, E 1953, The Norwegian Language in American: A Study in Bilingual Behavior. 2nd Printing, revised 1969. Bloomington: Indiana University Press, p. 5.

40 - Haugen, p. 5

41 - Lightbown, p80

42 - Harding & Riley, p. 5.

43 - Pinker p. 276.

44 - Pinker, p. 290.

45 - "More systematic evidence comes from the psychologist Elissa Newport and her colleagues. They tested Korean- and Chinese-born students and faculty at the University of Illinois who had spent at least ten years in the United States. ...The immigrants who came to the United States between the ages of three and seven performed identically to American-born students. Those who arrived between the ages of eight and fifteen did increasingly worse the later they arrived, and those who arrived between seventeen and thirty-nine did the worst of all, and showed huge variability unrelated to their age of arrival." Pinker, p. 291.

46 - Lightbown, p. 70.

47 - Pinker, p. 293-4.

48 - Lightbown, p. 72.

49 - Lightbown, p. 186.